'the other side of surfing'

contents

TRIBAL ELDERS (p.6): This story is the mainstay of this publication. Giving our respect back to the fathers of our sport is important in these times. Asking 11 legends of surfing their take on the industry, the future and generally seeking a passing of the knowledge to the next generation. A solid mix of individuals, from country kids to international superstars, their answers are quite diverse. From the old days, to board design, to the spiritual realms of surfing, this is a wealth of experience talking.

LEGENDS OF THE LENS: Much like the Tribal Elders, this story further immortalises the timeless images from days when surfing was innocent and pure, when style was common place and competition was primitve. From the father, Jack Eden, to the mid 1970's these images are classic pieces for any surfers home and I hope people get behind this venture to support these artists. All of these images are available at the website.

DICK VAN STRAALEN (p.94): Profile of a surfer/shaper who has always been the leader in innovative vibration shaping. Currently Dave Rastovich is a topic of many an interesting surf-craft, and you will learn more about how this symbiotic relationship thrives, with Rastovich and DVS both learning from each other. Tune in to find out how/why DVS is also a tribal elder and read more about the country life of the early 1970's and also, what DVS is up to today.

PETER DROUYN (p.186): One of the original 'outsiders', Drouyn has an important link to surfing's evolution in power surfing and also the competitive formula he devised at the first Stubbies Contest in 1977 one of the most successful surfing events in history. Bob Mctavish's revelation that Drouyn was instrumental in the shortboard revolution is news to the surfing world and leads to him being further acknowledged for the transition to the shortboard, along with Ted Spencer.

GEORGE GREENOUGH: Behind the scenes (p.36): George Greenough adds something from the future with his unique flair as a waterman and creative genius. Greenough talks beyond Dolphin Glide in this story, which focuses on Greenough the cinematographer, but also looks at some interesting projects he is working on today. George is a major contributor in this publication and I hope people enjoy more of a behind the scenes look at the real Greenough.

THE ART OF JAMMIN' (p.52): Music is an integral ingredient into this presentation, although it isn't a 'music' magazine. This story talks to several 'surfer musicians' to feel what the similarity is with getting tubed and jammin' and the sense of timelessness that is experienced. This story is also the launching platform for 'Low Pressure Sound Systems,' which is a collective of talented musicians who are following on from what Greenough and 'The Farm' started in 1970.

GLASS LOVE (p.80): A new movie by Andrew Kidman. From the maker of 'Litmus,' Kidman is a modern day Albe Falzon. This movie focuses on the father and son relationships of the Curren family and the Purchase family, with the soundtrack done by Kidman and friends.

SKETCH HOLIDAY (p.70): This book could have been an art magazine. Sketch Holiday is a talented cat and his input to this movement is important. Like the Art of Jammin', I hope the story on Sketch encourages artists, musicians and others to get involved with Switch-Foot.

RETRO REVIVAL (p.136): Talking to the leaders in surfboard design, we discuss the recent explosion in surf-craft that trim.

WOOD IS GOOD (p.112): Tom Wegner has a passion for surfboards that last a lifetime. Made from Paulownia timber, I can't help but feel we should all have one, but for construction expense. Also on the website we have info of bamboo, balsa, aluminium and carbon surfboards for anyone interested in sustainable materials.

SURF TRAVEL CAPTIONS (p.150): Anthony 'Yep' Colas is one of a very select crew of hardcore surf explorers. While this story only covers a dozen countries, there is more information on the website, with links to his famous 'Storm Riders Guide'.

NIGEL ARNISON / ON SURFARI (p.118): With a passion for photography, Nigel Arnison is one artist from a new school of artist talent that focuses on the artistic realms of imagery. This book would not be here without his passion.

photo : johnWITZIG

SURFINGS

TRIBAL **ELDERS**

Surfing (and beach culture in general) is close to the heart of many Australians and something that needs to be nurtured. Australian surfers need to learn from the Hawaiians and the way they respect their elders. Our younger surfers need to encourage the elders and embrace their naturally evolved style, not drop in and paint the wave with their adolescent immaturity/aggression and impatience.

These older surfers have been through the stage that many surfers are at, and that is the whole proving yourself in the water to both yourself and your peers. Some of the surfers in the water have been surfing for 40 years or more, some of them have been through hell and back and are still surfing. Have respect. The older surfers are a wealth of knowledge and that is one thing truly lacking in Australia...an understanding of our surfing history and who made our 'sport' what it is today. There are massive changes occurring in the surfing industry (as we read this) and what a good time to talk to some of the legends/elders of Australian surfing and ask them what they think! The change is an attitude shift and Bob McTavish describes it beautifully.

"The whole attitude towards surfing is changing. Instead of being the whole pro thing and everyone plugged into a strictly thruster mentality, there is definitely a much broader attitude going on today" (McTavish)

While there are changes happening and freedom of expression is encouraged (particularly in what type of board you ride), what a perfect time to introduce new ideas. Embrace the change and get the wheels in motion towards things that need to happen, particularly embracing the maturing nature of our beloved and shared passion that is, surfing.

It would be ideal if I could have interviewed about 50 legends of Australian Surfing but you can understand that this was a tough gig. I am pretty stoked to have words from the following gentlemen of the surf and I hope you enjoy reading their take on surfing.

CURL

1. Bob McTavish: Never a fan of competitive surfing, always innovating with his designs. Huge contributions to surfing, particularly with board design. Bob is an all around nice bloke, a family man, a businessman and an avid preacher of the Kingdom. Still hanging ten and getting stoked.

2. George Greenough: Originally from Santa Barbara in the States. I doubt anyone would claim to have contributed more to surfboard design than this man. His ideas have been taken and permutated right up to the modern boards and fins we use today. Learn your surfing history and you will learn how George impacted short boarding and surfing photography. Maker of the classic surf film, "The Inner Most Limits Of Pure Fun," George's current projects include the revolutionary new movie "Dolphin Glide" and "Behind the Scenes" that are both featured in this publication.

3. Peter Drouyn: One of the fathers of Queensland competitive surfing. Drouyn has been largely unheralded for his achievements in surfing, until this publication. He introduced the man-on-man competitive framework at the first stubbies contest in 1977, won numerous surfing titles including the Makaha international and Australian titles.

4. Nat Young: World champion several times over and the top surfer in his day. Father of Beau Young, who is also a world champion. First Aussie to rip in Hawaii! While being featured in countless surfing movies, Nat is also a successful author and part-time movie producer himself.

5. Peter Townend: First ever world professional surfing champion in 1976. Style master, "Bronzed Aussie" and 'coolie' kid, who despite being adopted by America and the big surf companies, is an Aussie at heart. PT is doing a better 'cutty' tomorrow than the one he did today!

6. Chris Brock: Underground cult hero who still surfs everyday. "Brocky" features heavily in many classic surfing movies including Albe Falzon's film "Morning of the Earth" George Greenough's "Inner Most Limits of Pure Fun" and also the classic "Free Ride." Good mates with George Greenough, whom he sailed on 'Morning Light' with. Brocky has made significant contributions to surfboard design and surfing in general.

7. Mark Richards: Four times world champ, the master of twin fin surfing and still shaping boards today. The 'wounded seagull' has a style in surfing, a unique style that we should all learn from.

8. Jim Banks: One of the original explorers and soul surfers of the 1970's. JB still lives the surfing life, shaping boards, jamming, doing yoga and having a positive take on surfing. A family man, who still explores the islands and still gets tubed.

9. Wayne Bartholomew (Rabbit): 1978 world champion, head of the ASP and one of the original 'coolie' kids. Rabbit busted down the door and rose to the top. Still surfing and still ripping in the surf and on the dance floor!

10. Dick Van Straalen (DVS): Master shaper who has had an underground cult following for nearly 40 years. Great surfer, innovator, lateral thinker and a family man... Currently involved with Dave Rastovich and shaping some very interesting surf craft for all kinds of surfers.

11. Midget Farrelly: First World champion in 1964. Midget made huge contributions to surfing in Australia and around the world. His breakthroughs in board design have not been fully appreciated to this day and he is not one for self-promotion.

If you think about what surfing was back in the late 1960's or even the early 70's and you compare that to the way the industry is today, do you like the way it has gone so far?

Peter Townend: "Oh, I think it is unreal. I mean I was one of the ones. We were the epitome of making a lot of noise, the Bronzed Aussies. We were the ones that went around saying 'a million dollars, we want to make a million dollars' well here we are now...and guys are!! (Much laughter)....We didn't, but they are! And you know, I don't have any bitterness about that or anything. I'm so stoked to see, the Fanning's and course Slater and Andy Irons and all these guys getting paid well for how well they surf, I think that's unreal. And to know that I was part of that I get a sense of pride with that you know....I dig it....I think it's gone the right direction and the guys do get paid...um...what it's worth..."

Brocky: "If you're talking about the industry, it's just what people get out of it, what they want to get out of surfing. Well when I was young, the only way you could live as a surfer was by being involved in the industry, making boards or something. It was something you just did, so that you could surf. But then as people wanted more material things, to get married and have families whatever, I guess guys had to make it more of a job where they are getting a wage just to support all the things like that. That's why I've always shied away from having a family and things like that, I wanted to enjoy life for what it was and what I like doing in life."

Rabbit: "My whole thing...it's still the good old days. That's my take on the whole thing. It's a totally personal experience, for me it's still the good old days. I do think that was a wonderfully golden era, but I think this is too. I don't live in another time zone, I live right now, and I'm really learning to enjoy the moment. You've got so much accessibility to other remote places, and you can still find waves."

Jim Banks: "Not mainstream no. There was something about the 70's...there was purity and there was the dream, and the adventure, and there was the counterculture aspect. It was like shove society, shove the nine to five, shove the rules.... we're just going to follow our hearts, treat each other well, eat well and enjoy the ocean. It was not for money and it wasn't for fame...that's what we're gunna do...purely because that's what our hearts want to do. That was amazing."

Bob McTavish: "It's been a bit of an avalanche, the pro thing and the marketing of surfing has sort of devoured it. It's something that got out of control you know...I reckon...and the soul has naturally been diluted...there's not a lot of soul in a 6"1 thruster."

Nat Young: *"Not honestly, no I don't. I'm one of those people who could have been a strong steering point at one juncture there. I really had some sort of control and people were asking me for a definition of what surfing really was and I said that it was an art form. It's sort of like it's hypocritical anyhow, because if it's an art form then you really can't judge it. You can't judge it on that level saying that the best surfers are the ones who win the contests.*

I go along with where we've got to. Where we have got to is that it's a fantastic sport that millions of people around the world really enjoy, and do mainly for the lifestyle. That's where it is, and you can't sort of say... woulda, coulda shoulda."

"You can walk into a large shortboard factory these days and you will see 50 stands with 50 clear glass jobs as the day's production, and they're all basically the same except for the slightly different logo or position... you know there's no real... they are almost machine made...there's not much variety, there's not much soul, there's not much individuality."

Drouyn: "I suppose there is a good side, a good evolutionary statement. Since the stubbies (1977), since the man-on-man at least the competition has become fairer. And by the way, the man on man system created the star system; the stars were born from the man-on-man, which created the image, which created the money."

George Greenough: *"Well not really, it's just gone this whole big competitive thing with massive promotion behind it. Surfing is something you go to do for fun with your friends isn't it?"*

Elder's

photo : johnWITZIG

What would you have liked to see if you had control over the direction of the surfing industry from the late 60's until today?

Van Straalen: "I would not have had contests. Maybe have festivals and let them be expression festivals so people can put forward their form of expression."

photo : dickHOOLE

Brocky: "There are so many guys who would like to live the lifestyle, tried to live the lifestyle, things didn't go their way, their missus left them, and they got nothing... fucken like Kevin Platt died living on his own in a caravan in Casino. So if I was Gordon, and I've got this bulk of money, from an industry that is made from surfing, they're giving just one person a million dollars a year and things like this, why not trap a little bit of that. It's getting a bit late with land prices and everything. But feed a bit of that on to buy some property and have an *old surfers' home*. Have a commune lifestyle that really should be lived by people. The thing is, surfers to me, they were one with nature, and for me, in a lot of ways they blazed a lot of paths. I mean Rabbit said that they were really the grandfathers of extreme sports. So instead of just turning into an industry like what's happening with it, with big money concerns on the stock market and all that, why not go back to the basics of how we really wanted it to be. Like in ya morning-of-the-earth years you know. I can't see why people don't do stuff like that when they get these big wealths of money. It's not that much to do, especially if you get a group of people together who will make it happen after the land's been bought. Imagine the publicity they'd get with stories and all that."

George Greenough: *"Wouldn't be any competitions I'll tell you that.* It would be people getting surfboards and going out and having fun. Hopefully there wouldn't be the aggro part we are having now. There are too many people around for the amount of waves; it's the same all over the world. I know people who have travelled around, and paddled out at some spot they've never seen anyone else out in the water, and they've got death threats just for paddling out, without even catching a wave."

Nat Young: *"I would have put it much more into a performing art syndrome, with governments taking responsibility and seeing the big picture for having....almost the way NIDA is, the National Institute of Dramatic Art. It's set up to foster talented artists doing their thing. Then you would have kept it right away from commercialism as you know it today, and it would have been regarded much more as an art form."*

Banks: "That's a big one. I think just more balance in presenting the whole spectrum of surfing. *I think that too much attention and too much focus, and too much money got thrown at the whole competitive professional thing.* That really limited the growth and the potential that surfing had. I always saw surfing as much more of a rock and roll show than as a contest. Some days I'd rather watch one guy go straight than another guy do ten turns. Some guys are just much more fun to watch going straight."

photo : peter CRAWFORD

"silence is the true friend who never betrays." [confucious]

Photo: jackEDEN

Right now it appears that the masses are starting to accept and embrace innovation in surf-craft again, have you noticed more and more interesting boards entering the water recently?

Brocky: "Since boards got so paper thin, and don't go in everything, kids are pulling out anything from out of the house, and having more fun than they would on their performance boards that day. And when it's cracking they pull out their performance board."

PT: Well it's not as experimental. It's nowhere near as experimental now as it was back then....you don't see.....I mean everyone is on a thruster now...back in the 70's you would have guys on a single, a twin fins fricken 4 fins...you know every type of different design shape you could possibly think of! But now if you line up the world's top 44 boards they all look pretty much the same within you know by a quarter of an inch, the only thing that is changing dramatically right now is in the construction...the moulded surf tech phenomena...is clearly having an effect.

Drouyn: "People are much more willing to stick their neck out and ride something different from their peer group. Before you were called an idiot. That's happening perhaps because a lot more surfers are a little bit older. Once you hit 28 in those days you were called an old man. Because surfing has matured as a participant regime. You've got guys who are not in competition anymore, and they'll make something different so they can enjoy it. There's a mixture of that, and the fact that the current shape has been around for so long now and it's grinding down to a halt. People just want a change, that's human nature. That's part of it, there's a combination of things.

There is a contradiction if not a hypocrisy. I've just talked about a very independent thinking generation at the moment, but it's actually not right. The masses are in fact becoming more robotic, and wanting exactly the same as what Fanning etc have and think that is all they should do. It's only a smaller community that are doing all this differential innovation or concepts or recycling old things and mixing things like recipes. I find that they are mainly your more mature gentlemen of the surf, who have been around a lot longer. We are in the generation where our poor kids are just brainwashed and marketed, it's shocking. There's a contradiction in surfing like that. Provided one of them uses one of those funny looking boards in one of the major contests and wins it. That's what's gotta happen."

Banks: "In the last five years I've noticed it...Guys starting to grab the old single fins out of the garage to go surfing on."

McTavish: "Hell yeah, heaps, the last two years has been an explosion of interesting boards. Not just straight retro but versions and variations that are very exciting."

Greenough: I think a lot of people are getting sick of just riding a thruster, and are starting to ride older boards they found at garage sales, and going wow this has got an interesting feel about it. That's where it's coming from. A 6'2'', 18 inch wide thruster that is 2" thick doesn't suit everybody. A weekend surfer who weighs 85 Kilos, he is gonna be struggling on it, he's gonna be floating up to his tits on it. Bigger older guys want an easier board to ride, particularly if you are heavy.

photos : dickHOOLE

' the stone that the builder refuse, will always be the head cornerstone.' [Bob Marley]

Elder's

Rabbit: "Always, I think just by the fact...it's a rare occasion for me to thrust myself into the ocean on my board and within ten seconds not be smiling, and not be going yahoo, I'm doing it again. I think I get even more stoked! I think as a grommet you're buzzing and it's all new and it's just unbelievable. You nearly like feel someone's gunna stop me soon, someone's gunna pull me up any minute here. Now it's like, I'm more appreciative. I appreciate that I'm still lucky enough to be in one piece and still be able to go out there at a certain level. It's important personally for me to surf really really well at 50, it's a very personal thing."

McTavish: "Oh yeah, absolutely I get stoked. It takes different things to stoke you. Now it's uncrowded, on the beach, usually with my wife and my dog and no one around, a nice little break and no one there, I'm out by myself. You're just as stoked. When I first started I was 15/16 you'd be stoked at anything, but now I'm a bit more selective. The same thing stokes you, it's the virginity of the break and of the experience. It's FRESH y'know, and that's what stokes you, is the freshness and the wonder of creation. You feel so special and spoilt to have that."

"Because the creator of the universe and the creator of this planet made things for us to enjoy...yes, it's a spiritual experience in that I'm appreciating the creators handy-work, and his love for us."

Brocky: "The way I look at it, life is so short so enjoy the pleasures of life. You've been given a gift, and you're lucky enough to be able do it. So why throw them things away when they are there and pursue something that really is only.... to pursue wealth and houses and things like that. It's really just a perception you have of how its gunna be for you. But for that perception to become reality...it very rarely becomes reality."

Banks: "For me, in the right conditions it is very spiritual, sure. There is something where I just, a sense of feeling really connected, if it's the right sort of surfing. Usually it's by myself because that allows me to just get out of my mind and not be chattering, not be socialising, just totally focused on connecting with the wave and feeling the texture of the water...feeling my board underneath me.... zooming right in."

PT: "Yeah, I mean it's...your first ride...even now I am in my 50's the ride I get tomorrow is just as stoking as the first ride! I mean it hasn't changed. And I still think I am gunna surf better tomorrow than I did today...even though I am getting older, I've still got my little boards and I think I am going to do a better cutback than I did yesterday! You know and it is addictive like that...even as you get older you still think you can get a better high tomorrow!"

Do you still get as stoked as when you were a grommet? And is surfing a 'spiritual experience' for you given the right conditions?

Greenough: "Hard to say let's see, my spiritual, or my religious experience... My parents took me to Sunday school when I was about four or five years old with my little brother. I can't really say because I don't know really what the word (spiritual) means. I don't have the... I don't have any religious backing. I had a great surf today, you saw the surf I was riding. One other guy came out; he didn't even wear a wetsuit out on the boogie. We were riding the wave right in the corner of the cape, about maybe a foot high."

Nat Young: "I would love to say I still get as stoked as when I was a grommet...but those days when you're just learning something, it was just so incredible and exciting... you stay out in the water all day...you miss your meals...you come in on the beach and lie on the sand all surfed out trying to warm up. When you're learning, you just want to do it all the time...I still have days when I lose sleep thinking about the quality surf in the morning and yes I still get stoked, but it's a different stoked to when you are a kid and it's all new and exciting."

"From my point of view I would define spiritual experience as feeling at one with God (if there is a God)...or feeling at one with nature (if nature equals God as Tom Blake outlined in 'Voice of the Atom'). *Essentially from my experience so far, definitely surfing can be a religious experience. Because I think there are times (when you're surfing) that you feel as close to nature as you're ever going to feel on this planet...*and if you're consistently in a position to place yourself in the tube...firstly you're going to pass through time... and those serious barrels (consistently) can transcend you to a space that I would say would be a spiritual experience, as close as I can imagine you can come to a religious experience. I haven't had a good tube for a year, but I know what it feels like and I sort of like the fact it doesn't happen to me all the time these days, 'cos it makes it more special when it does happen."

Drouyn: "Oh god, well absolutely. The spiritual thing, I don't know what it is, whether it is something we imagine inside our heads, or something to do with the environment, or it's just this notion of freedom...because it seems to me, anyone who is not free, in a sense it's hard for them to find spirituality."

Banks: "Come to think of it competitive surfing has probably contributed more to board design than anything else. So in that sense, it's been fantastic because it's really pushed the limits. Whether that would have happened without competition is speculation, I mean without competition, surfboard design is revolving anyway...so who knows they may have evolved just as fast...they may have evolved faster, and more diversely. I think the competitive thing really made people hone in on.... this amount of rocker...this amount of thickness...that sort of rail.... this type of concave...that sort of plan shape to get to this level of performance."

Nat Young: "I think that competition was a pretty good yardstick as far as proving your point to a lot of people who didn't think there was any validity to it."

Greenough: "That's a real hard... I suppose they designed surfboards for what the judges wanted to see. Everybody has got the Kelly Slater models now. They are basically built along that line. It was Tommy Curren before that, basically the sharp pointy nose thruster. You know, it looks aggro out in the water. It looks aggressive. That's what the people want, that's the look the judges want. Despite that, it would surf better if they cut the pointed end off of it...because they'd get rid of the extra swing weight, and the extra wind resistance."

Van Straalen: "It stagnated it. It stagnated it completely, it did. They all had to ride the same things because it's a system and they made them do that. I saw that in the first stubbies, when Michael Ho went out on this little board, and he was just going everywhere. They were just going Jesus, and they didn't know how to judge him. He was doing three turns down the face, and they were calling them wiggles instead of turns. He got robbed, most phenomenal surfing I've ever seen. It was so advanced for the time. (That was a Brewer). Michael and I went in and we made him a bunch of boards that went really good. That was the best thing about the stubbies, international people that were open. Today I find, because the nature of surfing has changed so much and all these people are getting paid so much. To get in there, you have got to pay 'em, to ride your boards. They are not riding boards because they like riding them; they are riding boards because they are getting paid to ride them. It's like endorsing products."

PT: "Oh it's been critical to surfboard design. ALL of the major changes, you know in the last 40 years have come as a result of competition...I mean we wouldn't have the thruster if it wasn't for Simon trying to figure out how to beat MR! I mean that's the bottom line on it."

How do you think competitive surfing changed the evolution of surfboard design?

MP riding a contemporary thruster outline.. Circa 1977

McTavish: "It's got it down to a very narrow strict discipline; the average 6'2'' thruster is a very refined piece of equipment. It is the most advanced piece of equipment without a doubt. It can do more on a wave than any other product, but they are all so similar. There is no room for an extra square inch of fat. They are trimmed to be the leanest, meanest most efficient piece of machinery. Which, I think is wonderful. But it's just one way of surfing... it's the most popular way of surfing."

Rabbit: "It's an innate competitiveness. It's like the race to Mt Everest. It's just there so it has to be conquered. The quest for the perfect surfboard, the quest for speed to get an edge in a competitive environment, to master these beautiful waves that we are blessed with, it's brought out a very deep-rooted competitiveness."

Brocky: "Everyone's always after something different. I remember in the days when we were riding the nose, big logs, pre-64, and pre-65, before that. How exciting would it be to go all over the wave? That was the dream then. That's what has been achieved now; the guys are going all over the wave almost to the point where they dunno what to do next! But in the long run, the go is to make the wave. So what you do along the way...that's what you get the thrill out of anyway, making the wave. Not fucking up halfway down the line. I look at it as a dance, and something that is keeping me fit, keeping me at one with nature. It's a dance. When I teach surfing...as soon as the arms come up...a style appears!!!... A style is born."

Photo: steveCOONEY

'it was more of an artform in the seventies...now it's slash, bang, crash, see you next time.' [MP]

This is the **FIRST** Dorsal fin surfboard in Australia circa 65' by the late Algie Grudd

Nat Young: *"I think they go hand-in-glove with where it's all up to... consumerism...none of them are going to last, it's just like disposable nappies really....you can just get another one.*

In the early days with surfing, we really had to nurture and look after our surfboards and you became close to them...especially the good ones, because no-one else had one! I mean I was totally convinced that SAM was absolutely an identity that was possessed and that I had a communication with....that I created...he was my mate you know and we did it together you know. I don't think it was an illusion either, I think that was the way it was meant to be, which is why he just disappeared. As soon as I became world champion he disappeared and I never saw him again, that's it gone. I think that's a wonderful thing."

"You can't compare that with these days all you have to do is make the phone call and there's another one exactly the same as the last one. There will always be room for the hand made shapers though."

Do you think the computer generated surfboards (being made today) are going to make hand-crafted boards extinct in the future?

Banks: "No I think we'll just see diversity. As far as the production goes the machines allow shapers to develop their designs quicker, spend more time fine-tuning and less time roughing it out and doing the crude stuff. It could give the true shapers more time and space to really hone in."

Van Straalen: "It won't affect it."

Rabbit: "Technology is happening all over the place. I don't know the answer to that, as far as the long-term effect, what's happening in China or what the new shaping technology...or just the whole mindset. It's definitely gunna change. There will be a choice whether to continue doing it the old traditional way or jump on the techno highway and go with it. That's just a very personal thing."

McTavish: "It will make this sort of thing (points to a hand-shaped McTavish Bluebird single fin) shine, without a doubt."

Drouyn: "It's a complex question, if I can simplify it. Using computer-generated images is ok but should only be used as a reference point, but not as actuality. The problem with clones is that it doesn't suit every individual. There might be a 1/84th mm that makes a board go different, or the weight of the guy, or the way he stands. There will always be a place for shapers. Anything that is handcrafted will win the day."

Greenough: "No, no, no way. A lot of people are gunna want that, but it's hard to get the individual shape though..."

Brocky: "Well it's gone mad, and it's gone... it's gunna go to the point. Talking to Steve Lis and Ben Aipa, all the Hawaiian shapers have got these models selling in the shops. What Steve said; 'If a kid breaks one of them in half, he can go and get exactly the same again!' So... that is a complete factory process. So that thing of a guy being able to live and surf and work/shape in the industry is slowly getting pushed out. Well, Tony Cerff said it to me a while back, you know... that computers could wipe out the shapers, and I said I have more faith in human nature than I have in humans' machinery!" (Laughs)

PT: "I have a theory. And hopefully it plays out this way.... we will never lose the artisan true craftsmen, like a Dick Van Straalen...you know the guy I learnt to shape under...and hopefully the polyester part of our business becomes where the design elements of surfboards happen and the prices go up...because surfboards today made by the traditional method...the polyester method, are too cheap!" (So hopefully the handcrafted boards will go up in value.)

photo of DVS: unknown

' a life is not important, except in the impact it has on other lives.' [jackieROBINSON]

How long do you think it will be until there is a mainstream surf craft that is 100% environmentally friendly in design?

PT: "I don't think... hmmm, it can't be viable you know... I mean the reason it can't be viable I just don't think technologically it's going to be better you know..."

Banks: "It's inevitable I think, it won't be long before there is no other choice. I think they'll be composite vegetable fibres, maybe timber. You can make resin out of sugar, almost anything in the garden you can make resin out of. That weed cow cane, I think would be ideal."

Van Straalen: "They are all environmentally friendly already. They are. Well I think the whole thing is that they are not environmentally friendly but they are. You got to remember that we can't make anything from nothing...so all these surfboards we have today have been made from organic matter. It all comes from the Earth; nothing can be created or destroyed. If we have made it into this toxic material, there must be a way of undoing that and returning it to organic matter. We haven't found that way yet, or they have found it but they are not telling us...everything is basically physics or chemistry."

Any scientific professors out there want a gig working out how to break down a modern surfboard back into organic compounds?

Greenough: "What do you mean, construction or what?I couldn't see it happening...what else...unless they go back to balsa wood and varnish, and then you can't get enough wood, there's no way they can obtain enough wood in this day and age. You could build a hollow wood veneer board, but still it's gunna take high tech construction vacuum bagging. He's probably gunna be using some kind of fibreglass mould to vacuum bag it in the shape of two halves."

Drouyn: "Yeah definitely. The authorities will soon get rid of chemicals and resin and people will come up with a whole new resin base that will do the same thing."

McTavish: "It will be very close, maybe not 100%, but very close, yes there's recyclable boards coming out using recycled materials, but there's still the fact that some of it ends up in landfill, it's not good."

Nat Young: "The moulded boards now seem to be getting very sophisticated. The ability to be able to make that product seems to be working quite well with where the surfing industry is up to...totally consumer orientated. Buy a board exactly like Slater rides, and buy a wetsuit exactly like Andy Irons wears. In the old days to get a good surfboard was.... you spent a lot of time and had a lot of duds, in order to find the right board. If an environmentally friendly board is going to happen, it hasn't happened yet."

Brocky: "I don't know anything about materials."

"Those materials when they are used, will involve mass production processes that will bring the costs way down. It will also put some factories out of business in the process. The machinery and technology involved is a different process entirely, that traditional surfboard shapers don't understand. That's coming... it's unstoppable. It's because of the demands of recycling, and because China and Thailand are already invading into the traditional handmade industry of the west. The next backlash is going to be a technology from the west which will seriously affect the Chinese and Thai industry."

surfer: early hawaiian and big wave pioneer......bobPIKE

Who are the most under-rated surfers/shapers in Australian surfing history in your opinion?

Rabbit: "*Drouyn,* his surfing hasn't been fully recognised. In some respects I'd even say *Midget,* because he was the first world champion. They all fell into the ominous shadow of Nat in many ways. *I think Midget's contribution is far greater than has been acknowledged.*

Another two who I think were amazing surfers were *Ted Spencer* and *Keith Paull.* They were pure stylists, amazing surfers, and amazing characters. People have probably never heard of these guys. Keith was a huge influence on our generation.

For *Gordon Merchant,* his other achievements have overshadowed it. He was a great shaper, a very innovative guy. What I saw at the Joe Larkin factory with Gordon, *Terry Fitzgerald, Michael Peterson,* it was amazing. *Dick Van Straalen* is a very innovative shaper. He's always looking at different things. He thinks outside the square, with a totally different approach. I rode some of Dick's boards in 71 for a period there. They were fantastic surfboards to ride. He's been happy to take that position."

Brocky: "There have been a lot of different people who have put little bits in here and there that people have grasped. For me, I grabbed... *George (Greenough)* with the double concave...and *Gordon MERCHANT* with the tucked under rail. Gordon was the first one to do the tucked under rail. He used to live in his Kombi van, he'd just come back from Africa, living at Elands Baii. He lived in a canvas lean-to there, and shaped boards. He was a goofy...there were a lot of people who put bits in that have never had part of it. I'd say probably whoever shaped Wayne Lynch's boards...might have been John Arnold...rolled bottom, wide point aft. I think he (Wayne) did some shaping himself."

Greenough: "Shit, I wouldn't know, I wouldn't have a clue. There are people out there screwing around with shit, out in the boondocks, someone who you don't even know."

Van Straalen: "There are heaps of them. I don't know. The thing I admire today is guys who are still doing it, and haven't bowed to pressure. There is a whole team out there who are still hand making surfboards. I admire that, because it isn't easy. Everyone is living their dream. These other guys, latest haircuts, latest cars...they are making 500-600 boards a week, what I make in a year! It's all show.

"If you really want to know... *Kevin Brennan.* He was phenomenal. When we first moved here (to Queensland 1969) he came with us. I was teaching him how to shape. He just had personal problems. In the end it got hold of him and it was too much. When he was growing up and he got a lot of shit from everyone, and it played on him, it's Hard Yakka growing up. Due to leg-ropes no-one switch foots anymore and Brennan was the master Switch-foot rider. I think there is some good footage of him surfing in Paul Witzig's film "Hot Generation" for example."

Drouyn: "One thing I've learned in life is that you may be called world champion and what have you, but somewhere someone could be doing exactly what you are doing, could be doing just as good as you are doing, but either don't have the opportunity or the resources or whatever. If I was to target some people...*Keith Paull* was never recognised for his shaping prowess. He was one of the greatest shapers of all time Keith Paull. He hit his peak around 1970, and it's so ironic that Rolf Arness, who won that 1970 world title/final.... Guess who shaped his board, Keith. In Hawaii the following winter I rode Keith's boards to all those victories. I bought Keith's boards off him, mine were no good so I bought his whole quiver, like 2 boards, in Hawaii, and rode them in the contests and never looked back. It is wrong Keith hasn't been recognised. There are lots of others."

PT: "Well I have a really personal attachment to one of them...*Dick Van Straalen....* you know I mean he has an underground cult following that's lasted 40 years! Hahaha..." (See our story on Van Straalen)

"I think people didn't realise what *Michael PETERSON* was doing, I mean stuff he was doing was revolutionary, where he was moving the curvature in the board long before...and the rocker things he was doing...no one figured out what the hell he was doing! What he was doing was kind of what Slater figured out with Al Merrick when they went in to the whole rocker thing with thin boards you know and they became you know as a result more like rocket ships.... and MP was kind of doing it back then!"

Banks: "There's so many. Maybe not underrated, but just didn't get the attention, for their level of ability. I grew up with them. There are a whole lot of us at Cronulla; all of them are as good as me. There's *Ross Marshall, Peter Smith, Craig Nala,* all those guys were every bit as good as me. I kind of got a lucky break, maybe had a little bit more desire, or belief that I could do it, it wasn't surfing ability. 'Under-rated surfers' are everywhere, you go to any beach, there are guys just ripping everywhere."

Nat Young: "It's difficult because quite a few of them are dead. *Keith Paull* was a real contemporary of mine; we competed a lot together and surfed a lot together. The big thing with Keith was, he had an incredible amount of talent, people don't really realise in this country, but in the States he was very commercial. He was doing it in order to make money to live. When I was working for Weber doing a real heavy push, he was working for Bing and giving it a real shove. We were in every town on the East coast selling boards. He was a very good salesman because he was so sure of what he was and so totally committed to being a quality surfer and a quality person. I don't know where exactly he came off the rails, he called my house a few years ago and unfortunately I wasn't there... I feel like I never really had a chance to give him any sort of love. That actually is a lot of my regrets in this activity; everybody seems to be so tangled in personal jealousies, and competition that it really fucks up a lot of people. The jealousies, that ugly side of surfing, I tend to think that it all came from competition. I guess the reason I don't have that was that when I was competing I was pretty successful."

McTavish: "Looking back in time? I got to say *Kevin Platt* in the 60's. It's a tough question. A lot of them have carved their niche. All the guys who really loved it and were really dedicated stayed with it, and they've all got themselves little slots somewhere in the industry if they loved it that much.

Definitely *Gordon (Merchant),* I had a talk with Gordon three months ago, I had to say to him the tucked under rail that you did in 73, in 71 there was a lot of it around. In 69 were the first tucked hard edges. He showed me a board from 71 with a beautiful tucked edge. We all did it on some boards, Dick Brewer did it on some boards, Hynson did it on some boards, Lopez did it on some boards, I did it on some boards. Gordon did it on every board, and he did it exactly right by 71."

"So yes, I'd say Gordon is underrated."

"I dunno, I'd like to answer this by saying that there are very few good designers. There had been a lot of shapers, today probably in Australia there are 1000 shapers. But, I don't think there are more than a handful of designers. A designer is someone who understands what's going on in a surfboard. A lot of shapers today don't have the opportunity; because all they see is a 6'2'' every time it comes off the planing machine. They don't get a planer and cut a rocker. So they don't understand why a board has a concave on that spot or what a bit of tail rocker does to it, or why that rail works so well. There are very few shapers who are actual true designers who understand how things work. So I really only have great respect for the ones who are shaper/designers."

Well what about in 20 or 30 years, who is going to be able to shape a board then with technology going the way it is going?

McTavish: "Fortunately we have the *Dain Thomas's* and the *Ben Mctavishs'*. They are the two I know right away who are here who can do that work. Dain is 25, Ben is 27, and they can do a board from start to finish. They want to understand the entire thing. They can do the whole lot. Fortunately there is a young generation of shapers coming through who are not interested in being pop-out, mass production shapers." (See our story Byron Subculture for more information on Dain Thomas and 'SEA' surfboards)

Random offcuts

Bob McTavish: If you think about it the longboard history only went from 56-67. It lasted 11 years, in the old time. It's nothing. Then the revolution came through maybe from 67-71, was the hot stuff. The basic ingredient of the modern surfboard had basically been done by 71, including three fins, low down rails, the rockers, the templates, the volumes. They'd all been done. So, for the last 30 years we've been fooling around with what had already been established, presented in 71. So the hottest period was 67-71. The second generation of longboarding is already 20 years old, it came out in the mid 80's.

AC: Do we have to go back and work with intricacies of the past

No, I still think the 6'2'' thruster is the most sophisticated piece of equipment. I think that if people ignore what's in there when they do modern designs they have to be very careful. There were a lot of things that were wrong, everything had been done properly in pieces by 71. But 99% of boards made did not reflect that, because they always had some built in problem. Usually it was the rocker, too stiff in the tail. Or it was rails being too dropped in the tail, which created a negative lifting force when you were doing roundhouse cutbacks. I don't think that any old design is necessarily good, some of them have their place though.

Brocky: That is why we made little stubbies. Because we were sick of jumping forward, and getting in the tube, and not really being able to turn to come out of the tube again. That's why we imitated George; he could do the roundhouse nice and set up for the next tube. You had to step back to do your turn, that's why we imitated George's boards. You'll see in morning of the earth, everybody's jumping forward. Even Michael Peterson.

If noseriding contests became popular, it would be really good for surfing to break away from that flick professional thing and get back to smooth basic stuff. To have a good noserider, you can't turn it with flick turns, it's the roll...like you're Joel Tudor style. It would bring back that beautiful...people can see that's beauty when they see it even if they don't surf...it's not the flowing thing it was years ago when I was young. Where it was the flow and that was a dance.... when I see that come out I get excited. I've probably had too many days on the South Coast when I was young. I just want beautiful waves, out in the bush, countryside, and no hassles. If somebody did make a farm...we could get back to the movie they've all embraced...where you did it to be free.

Nat Young: Essentially, the passion for surfing and the whole thing of riding waves has got little to do with the sporting professionals. It's got really to do with this compassion for riding waves that takes you to another whole...it's totally all encompassing in your life. We have to accept that ok, it didn't go down that track, here we are in this track, having it as a sporting activity, and how do we make that work best, for all of us. I don't think it's working too badly. You see a lot of smiling faces out in the lineup. There have been periods when it has been worse, now I don't see it as such... Now there is such an incredible broad spectrum of society involved in surfing we've got to really give them an education about what it is, because they don't know. When we were kids, the old guys all told us, this is the way it is. It is such an incredible big cross section of the community involved in surfing, and we really have to be much more giving, and much more understanding than we ever were in the past. That's not a bad thing, it's just the way it's got to be.

Peter Townend: We were more artists back then. We were more like a musician with a bunch of guitars... and we wanted to change the sound of our guitar... so we made 'em ourselves... you see that's the difference... they don't think like that now you know... like we would have a rack of guitars, where you would change the strings or you would tune it differently you know...

Rabbit: We were only just starting to work out what a fin was; this whole influence was coming in. We'd be onto what Wayne Lynch was doing down there in the wilderness of Victoria with his fins... and the George Greenough stuff...what Brocky was doing... and Nat and the keels. It was so exciting. Terry Fitzgerald and the little pivot fins... and sideslipping... man, it was something else. All these little components of the board...one week everyone is riding longboards, next week everyone's riding shortboards that are basically chopped off, rounded and glassed. Then came the design. We had these grand prix tracks out here... it dawned on me. You have your summer equipment and you have your season equipment. You have your summer really wide little things that you can do roundhouse cutbacks on at two foot onshore rainbow, and you have your cyclone season min-guns. It's a whole attitude shift. MP was definitely onto that one early.

I look to the kids, because they have that natural exuberance, that's the time when they have to have this instilled in their whole approach in surfing. They are the key, and they are so influenced. It is all in the whole nurturing process.

GG: I am more of a trimming, carving surfer rather than a snap surfer, making big snaps. Judges are impressed with how much water you throw up in the air. So boards have to be designed to throw water in the air. So you want hard edges. Real soft boards don't throw water as well as hard-edged boards. I tend to put concave in the forward part of the board to get it up on a plane quicker, and to get me across dead spots. But I like a rolled relief in the back of it, so when I get back in the pocket it's comfortable. When I came over here, I came over with completely different equipment. The first time I went to Noosa on a pretty big swell. Everybody has got their longboards and they are all going out at main beach, there's no one out at National Park, it's six to eight feet, it's offshore, it's perfect. I was straight up there surfing by myself. National park was a parking lot right there, you've been to Noosa. You got main beach, national park, tea tri and granites. When national park got big no one rode it, because it was very hard to ride with the equipment they had back then. They all had longboards, my equipment was like half the size of that they were using. Very agile, well proven design. They are looking at what I'm doing and going well fuck we want to surf like that, so they started making surfboards small.

AC: what year?

GG: 64/65 somewhere around there.

Lennox was another spot, as soon as it got big no one surfed it. There's all that push of surfing development. That's what pushed me a lot, dealing with the crowds. Like Rincon, it was called Rincon indicator, but it's just an extension of the pointbreak but bigger and faster and sectioning. If I could build a board to suit it I had an uncrowded surf spot. Now it's horribly crowded the whole way through the spot. You could ride waves other people couldn't, so you had surf on your own all the time. Have a look in echoes I was out there filming, look how many people you see in the background... you don't see anyone because there was no one out.

Keep experimenting with things, nothing ventured, nothing gained. You don't have a shot at it you won't know.

photo: georgeGREENOUGH

photo : dickHOOLE

' speak softly and carry a big gun.' [theodoreROOSEVELT]

As a tribal elder of surfing, do you have any advice you would like to share with the readers out there about surfing, lifestyle or anything else?

Rabbit: "It's an all engrossing activity and lifestyle, and that's what makes the surfing culture rich. You only have to think out of the box, with a bit of lateral thinking you can still find waves. If you have to be at the best spot on the best day, it is gunna be crowded, but there is lots of other surf around too. The whole accessibility of big wave riding, it's so exciting. I guess in some respects the elders get upset, it's hard for them to fathom. There was no one before them, they had complete control of line-ups. They do have a sense of ownership. That's when it breeds localism. There is a balance; you also have to have something that prevents a place from being completely over run. I have learned and got a lot out of my Hawaiian experiences, it's a whole different attitude over there. A guy like Rabbit Kekai for example...he's in his 80's, and still surfing, he's stoked. Peter Cole, he's still out at Sunset Beach at 70. It's a whole different thing. They'll ride anything; they'll ride longboards when it's small. They'll ride any craft and have fun. I'm getting more like that all the time. I don't worry about, 'you gotta stay in your box.' That's a bit of a negative Australian thing, that you've got to stay in this box as a shortboarder, or you gotta do this. I think you can learn a lot from the Hawaiians, when it's flat they'll get out a paddleboard and go paddling. They'll do anything. That's the essence that I'm trying to capture."

Brocky: "Just get as many go outs without any people. Just take it as it comes...go surfing and enjoy it for clearing your mind without trying to be better than someone else. I've talked a lot to George about little things like this. I love to see another guy get a good wave. I love seeing that. They say that in surfers the movie, right at the end they talk to Owl Chapman...he says...'Give a guy a wave, you never know, he could have a good looking sister!"

"One thing I say about all this, and the *&^%$ getting every wave, flicking it everywhere...I say have another one! 'cos in a few years you won't be here surfing...you'll be sore" (laughs)

McTavish: "Listen to Jehovah's Witnesses next time they knock on your door. Most Christian religions put us down but only because we are revolutionaries. We live for the modern era. The message is that God's Kingdom is coming."

Nat Young: "The thing that I think is a really great principle is hurry slowly. Even if you are turning a surfboard or walking down the street or if you are driving a car, you are going fast but you should be trying to do it with as much dignity, as much style, as much patience as you possibly can. *Finish what you start,* that's another piece of advice. In surfing it is a tribe, I really feel that we have a unique perspective in riding waves, and what we have got to do now is back right off trying to cut everybody's throats to get to the top. I'd like to think that's the way it could go. It probably won't because so far it hasn't. There's gunna be more waves, and you are going to get a few of them..."

Banks: *"I'd really like to see surfers embrace the concept more of surfing together, and not surfing against each other.* Lets not fight over them or hassle each other, I've done all that shit you know, and I'm reaching a point where, there are a lot of places I won't surf just because of how it is in the water. It doesn't matter how good the waves are, when I come back to the beach it leaves me with this feeling that just isn't what I want to feel. That was the damage that competitive surfing did, it created a mindset of everyone surfing against each other. It's a never ending heat. It's not the number of people in the water, it's the attitude of people in the water. I've been out at really crowded breaks, and it's so cool in the water because everyone is tuned to surfing together. This tends to happen in more remote places, out in the desert and stuff (People living together with a more communal feeling). I can go surfing down the beach here, and one guy will paddle out with only three of us in the water, and it's just hell. This one guy is just not tuned."

Greenough: *"Just basically try and keep the violence under control and try and be considerate of the other people in the water.* People have the attitude, 'oh that guy's a kook I'll drop in on him'.... That wave, that guy they are calling a kook, could be the best wave of that guy's life, and you've had a million waves just like that, why be greedy and take his? If people behave like that in the water, they are generally gunna behave like that on the land."

"The good waves, people like the point waves. You've got Broken Head, Lennox Head, Superbank, Kirra, they are all easy waves to ride. The waves run down a set bank. Most of the time, unless it's really big, it's easy to get out. It's easier, that's why they are so crowded. You ride a beachbreak and it's a hollow wave, it's got good bottom tension, your boards perform well, you go out on some flat-based wave that doesn't run off very well, or closeout beachbreaks, it's not as much fun, it's why everybody's going to those spots."

"I go surfing for fun, I'm not trying to prove anything to anybody. I haven't surfed Lennox any good probably for about, well it's gotta be at least 12 years. I just don't bother anymore; it's just not worth the hassle. Dealing with the aggro and the bad vibes the place has."

PT: "It's still about the thrill of the ride. Whether you're a grommet or a pro surfer, whether you're an old guy... or a 'tribal elder' (laughs) there is still nothing (that I know of) and I have experienced a lot, there is nothing that compares to it... it's like a natural drug. When you get that ride, you go, that was cool (laughs) and it's like an addiction... I gotta do that again! So I think at times everyone gets all too hung up on the competitiveness of it (and I don't mean the contests) I just think everyone should just lighten up a little bit! There's gunna be a lot more waves! They all keep coming! Storms aren't gunna stop happening! There's going to be another storm and that means more waves."

"For me now, being a bit older... when you're younger, you're more intense, more feverish... you gotta get more of 'em... these days, good sessions are measured by one good wave (laughs) If I get one good wave, I am fulfilled, I am happy... I got the ride!"

Van Straalen: "It's a spiritual experience. When you analyse the whole thing of what we are doing, it's pretty enlightening. You gotta think about what we are riding, we are riding a wave of energy. You look at the shape of it and actually gyro energy, and you are riding these little pieces of plastic, that are bent. It's phenomenal. You think about what's going through your mind when you are surfing, and it's pretty far out. It's a form of meditation. That's why you find a lot of people who are locked into surfing, not the aggressive side, and they are very peaceful people. They are very at ease with themselves and the world. It is something that is very special. You can't get it anywhere else. Mountain climbing, stationary, we are riding something that is moving. If you were to convert that energy the waves are into something, you'd have this giant electricity plant."

'You can imprison yourself with how you think about things. As people are growing older they imprison themselves by their thought patterns. My idea is that you look at this and you look at that and think 'I don't want to be like that' and so the whole thing is to free yourself from it... like I remember someone saying to me really early: "The only way to change your life is to change your thinking." And the other one was: "Everything is the way you think it is." And it is so true. By thinking all these things and being negative and critical you are creating this world that you've basically locked yourself in, so you really have to be free about how you think about things and not be critical of anyone, or try not to be critical and judgemental, because we are all basically the same. We are all blood and bone, our hearts beat the same, there is just so much of people criticising everyone and condemning everyone. Basically what I have tried to do is free myself from all that.'

Mark Richards: "With the popularity of surfing world wide crowded conditions are becoming a major problem. *I think it is really important that we have a tolerant attitude when we surf, everyone is out there just trying to ride some waves and have fun! Regardless of whether you are on a body board or a surfboard we're all looking for the same thrill - (to ride a wave!)* No one owns the ocean or a surf spot, a postal address near a surf spot does not give you ownership! Localism totally sucks, at some point we are all tourists; I think if we treated people the way we'd like to be treated the lineups would be less aggro and a lot more friendly."

Midget Farrelly: I don't really consider myself to be a 'Tribal Elder' because I always figured I was living on the outside and was never part of anything. Surfing always gave me something special in life and I didn't need to be part of what was 'normal.' If you like something and do it with passion then you will become good at it (naturally) and it will sustain you, but you have to find joy in it. If you get joy from it, then it will show."

Drouyn: "Always remember, past this point is freedom. Kids today are really stuck in a prison of marketing oppression. It is the marketing of corporatism that is killing our kids' ability to think independently and think creatively and use their imaginations. I think that is so sad, I almost want them to know, they are only surrounded by four lines and all they got to do is step through one of those lines and keep running.... because past that point is freedom of your mind and independence."

Conclusion from the editor: The words that come from all of these surfers, comes from experience. There are not many people reading this that have more experience in surfing than these guys and if we added up all the collective experience, we are talking hundreds of years of experience in surfing. Therefore, take their words as gospel. Having read, re-read, interviewed, phoned, surfed with and interviewed again, talked and had coffee and breakfast...having watched them in shaping bays, seen them at surfing functions and generally immersed myself in their presence in the last 12 months... there is one VERY clear message...you don't hear many of these legends raving about the beauty of the competitive side of surfing. In fact, most of them blame competitive surfing for the aggressive attitude of most surfers in the water today. The message is clear, take the aggression out of the art form. **AC**

photo : dickHOOLE
surfer: michaelPETERSON

' this is not the end. it is not even the beginning of the end. but it is perhaps. the end of the beginning.' [winstonCHURCHILL]

'The late fifties and early sixties were a special time for surfing. Great transitions were made in a sport that had been the obscure domain of the surf lifesaving movement. Suddenly new characters appeared in the surf. Surfing skills, dress, cars, music and attitudes were created that reflected a carefree, hedonistic lifestyle. If you wore jeans you were anti-social and if you rode a motorbike you were a bodgie. Then surfing came along with the clothes, music and image and helped break down barriers. All too soon this special decade had vanished and it wasn't until the nineties that the real value of the time was realised. Luckily, Jack Eden caught many of the major players of this era on black and white film. His precision images truly convey the uniqueness of a never to be repeated pioneer period in Australia's surfing life.'

MIDGET FARRELLY

one. Jack Eden the 'Godfather' of Australian surfing photography. two. Makaha tandem finals, Hawaii. 1964. three. Bobby Brown, Sandon Point, Bulli. 1964. four. Butch Cooney, Newcastle Championships. 1965.

five. Final Wave, Midget Farrelly [winning] at the first World Championships, Manly. 1964. six. Femlin, Kirra, QLD. 1963.

email enquiries to: enquiries@mediacentre.com.au

one. On Surfari at Voodoo. two. Kevin 'The Head' Brennan, hangs ten, Manly. 1965. three. Kevin 'The Head' Brennan, North Avalon. 1964. four. Phil Parkinson, Bellambie. 1964. five. Big Guns, Long Reef. 1964.

. Bottom Turn, Bobby Brown. 1965. . Soul Surfer, Burleigh Heads. 1962. . Midway, Gary Birdsall, Cronulla Point. 1959.

Enquiries to: Jack Eden ph +61295298688

Dolphin Glide
" we keep passing unseen through little moments of other people's lives." [robert.T.PIRSIG]

George Greenough "behind the scenes"

AC: When did your passion for getting out into the water with a camera begin?

GG: My father had a wind-up 16mm magazine camera (the equivelent to a super 8mm) and that's what I started screwing around with, and I have a few bits and pieces from then that will go into 'behind the scenes' (Georges next project) and really look at the history of the photography and stuff and kind of the ideas and concepts behind the whole thing.

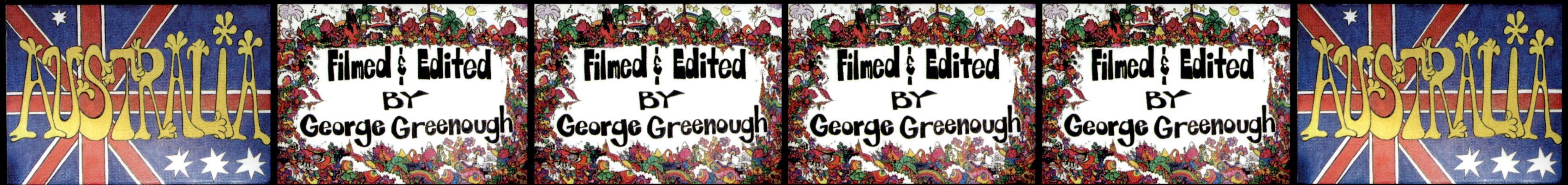

AC: Who do you hope will like your film, Dolphin Glide?

GG: Mainly it is designed as a general audience film. It is an experience film...if they want to see what a dolphin experiences, then this is the film to see. It is a pleasant experience, it takes your mind off things. I don't have an advertising budget for it though and I am not very good at selling the idea to someone, I am more of a producer. I like getting the material and putting it together.

AC: How many soundtracks did you make before you chose the right sound to go with this quite unusual material?

GG: Really just one. Eventually the film, when it is finished we are going to have two other soundtracks. So we've got the middle of the road one that's one there now, then there is going to be an ambient one and a more up-beat dance style one. So if you want a laid back soundtrack with light shows and stuff, then you choose the laidback one, if you want more energy in the soundtrack then pick the high energy one.

AC: You have finished Dolphin Glide, where do you see people being able to watch it?

GG: It showed around to some degree in theatres, and again, I don't have an advertising budget so we didn't get much of a showing out of it in theatres, but it did well here in the local town of Byron Bay. Maritime museums and amusement parks could be a possibility. I am a producer, I produce these things...I am not good at getting it out there for people to buy or whatever, that is a job for a distributor.

AC: What about discovery channel?

GG: Television is like baby food...they want everything pre-digested. Dolphin Glide is an experience film, like coming of the dawn and echoes and I don't think you will see any of that type of material on TV.

AC: The making of Dolphin Glide really goes a long way to explaining how you captured the footage

GG: Dolphin Glide required much larger cameras, because it was shot on super 35mm and I was using a Mitchell (I didn't have the latest light weight camera you can get in Hollywood hahah) the camera I used was built in 1951 for the US military and it was very heavy and robust, the same camera they used for filming

rockets...an extremely well built camera. I was body surfing with that camera, to capture the material. I had to modify it so that it pierced through the water easily when I was body surfing, and I used the same camera on a rig I built for the boat, so I get a very good seamless inter-cutting between the two.

AC: If we talk about 'coming of the dawn' you basically built the camera with the water housing and got out there and shot this deep deep tube riding experience in 1969-70, when surfers were not even really tube riding yet.

GG: That was the hard part, going out and shooting it...because at that time, I knew virtually nothing about cameras. Back at that age, you are basically young and dumb and you will go out and charge anything. So, I'd go out with 25 pounds of camera gear on, I had two lead-acid batteries, they weighed 12 pounds in an inner tube around my waist, and a very heavy (war surplus) camera and housing on my back and I would go out there and go over the falls until I got a wave that I could finally get going on. That's how that whole thing started and I was just learning more about it and I was able to get the weight down, until I finally got it down around 15 or 16 pounds, that is what the rig weighed... mainly by getting rid of the lead-acid batteries and getting nickel-cadium batteries. Still difficult to surf with, you still had plenty of trips over the falls trying to get waves on the spoon with it.

AC: Do you think surfers had realised you could get that far back into the tube before they saw coming of the dawn?

GG: Well, the big problem I found out of course, was that the camera only saw what was in front of you. The camera angle is deceiving and doesn't really show how far back a tube ride may be. I've got a shot, that is a known shot, and crew on the beach said 'oh that was a great shot, you completely disappeared for two seconds and came out'...now I know that wave and that shot, when I came into the beach I said it wasn't deep enough and I don't even think the shot will make the film. I was completely out of sight, I was back that far and the shot didn't make it into the film. But it will make it into the next film 'behind the scenes' because I will use it as an example to show when I do a shot, how much deeper I was. The big tube that was in 'Echoes, I mean that was basically as far back as you could get and still come out. It was very difficult with the camera only seeing what is in front of you, plus dealing with the weight of the camera and you have to, ideally, surf for the camera.

Greenough

AC: A bit about behind the scenes...

GG: The new project is basically more behind the scenes, more how the spoons work in the surf, and the same thing with the fins and things...modifying swim fins, modifying board fins to get better performance out of it. How do you foil and tune a fin for better performance, that sort of thing. Doing photo analysis and also getting into deep tube riding, where you can do frame by frame analysis of it. Like, in the computers now you can slow things down very easily, you can step print it, you can zoom in and out of various aspects and I can stop it and talk about part of it and then move on and stuff. That is kinda the concept behind it. Some of it will be more about the experience of surfing, and that will be more up to the musicians to do it, and you might have two or three different soundtracks on that, to get different people's opinions on it...and I wouldn't call it rap music or hip hop, it is more an old blues style like Albert King or something.

AC: Like the Farm?

GG: Yeah exactly

AC: So you are working on mostly old off cuts for your next project, Behind the Scenes or is it new footage?

GG: Basically it is all gone back through the old material. Obviously all the best shots made it into the movie ('The Inner Most Limits of Pure Fun') but I have also found some really interesting material in there. My big problem doing this (talking about the performance aspect of the spoon) is that there isn't any material of the spoons really being pushed to the limit in big surf that is shot from the beach...I mean not that I have been able to come across. I've got a lot of material that I found shot on-board (stuff I shot myself with the camera on my back) that I can use that was shot in large surf though.

AC: Do you think at the moment with experimental board design experiencing a renaissance, that maybe we will see the spoon coming back at all?

GG: Difficult to say, but they may use the same ideas. I will not only be talking about the spoon, I will also be talking about the windsurfers, which are larger. They vary from 6'7" to 7'3" and are also a spoon set up.

AC: When did you build your first windsurfer?

GG: about 1981

AC: How many have you gone through to get to this high performance model you ride today?

GG: There are quite a few around. The early ones were obviously just a big slab, just a big floater. You had to pull the sail up. It's not like I windsurf constantly. It's just another water toy, you have a lot of fun with. I guess, it's like having a jet ski or something.

AC: What are some of the features of your latest windsurfer?

GG: It is very similar to what the spoons are. It is just a big spoon with a windsurfing rig put on it to drive it.

AC: It's not flexible is it?

GG: Yeah it is. They are all flexible. That's the whole concept behind the thing, it has variable rocker in it. That's where the windsurfer would be more interesting to look at the design, because it is larger craft and people will be able to relate to it.

AC: Where does the variable rocker really come into its elements?

GG: Well variable rocker gives you GIVE. In other words, if you want to turn sharper, the board... you induce more rocker into the board, because the board flexes. And it is a designed-in flex, it's not just a rigid curve. In other words the rocker produces a parabolic curve to increase the acceleration out of turns and things. It's like suspension on a car, imagine if your car had no suspension. It goes around corners better and sticks it to the water.

AC: Have you ever tried tow-in surfing?

GG: Well basically, using the windsurfer is the equivalent of that. If you look at the board, the spoon is 18 1/2" wide by 7'3" long, it is slightly larger than what a tow-in board would be and instead of using some kind of a power boat to tow it onto a wave, I have a very sophisticated double surfaced sail that serves the same purpose. The sail is designed basically so that when you let the power off the sail, it goes absolutely neutral. In other words, it has no pull at all. So I can use the sail to catch the wave, and to surf the wave I use the spoon. The big disadvantage though is the 14 and half foot mast, which makes riding the tube almost impossible. It would be fairly simple to design a system where you could remove the sail when you have caught the wave and throw the rig away and you could put a bladder in the sail, so it would float and wash in...but then of course the main disadvantage with windsurfing and taking lots of chances is that...things will break! The most vulnerable part of it is the sail. You know if it gets beat up enough it will rip...and due to the fact I make my own sails, then I've got to make another sail. So, I don't take a lot of risks windsurfing.

AC: People send you lots of surfing movies...do you watch any of them?

GG: Some of them I do. I've got the latest issue of Tracks Magazine and it had a Quicksilver freebie, three hours of thrash and crash, I haven't turned around and looked at that but certainly ones I get from Andrew Kidman and people like that I look at it. Some of them are really interesting to watch.

AC: Most of the footage from 'behind the scenes' is from the 60's. Are you going to touch on the whole transition phase of the shortboard revolution?

GG: To a minor degree. I don't think I am going to make a big deal about it. To a minor degree, there will probably be some discussion. Basically you can see, I mean I have got all the material in there of what happened. What would you think of 1966 watching Andy McAlpines film 'Children of the SUN' and you see me riding the spoon at National Park Noosa and what I was doing on the wave compared to what people were doing on longboards. I mean, what would you think if you walked up the beach and you were Bob McTavish or Nat Young or something like that. I'd be starting to screw around with surfboards, going shit, there is a whole new thing happening out there. Of course when it came along to filming, inside the tube, people were still in the transition phase and I was already getting that material. Once I figured out the camera gear, it started happening. But it's not like today with video, that is not only lighter and easier to use, but you can get it home, plug it into your TV and look at it and see what you've done wrong, so the learning curve is much quicker and it doesn't cost you anything compared to shooting film.

AC: How many surfing contests have you gone in George?

GG: None. I've gone in windsurfing speed trials, it was a lot of fun, because you were racing the clock. It was back in an era when it wasn't heavily sponsored. I was only two thirds of a knot off the winning speed, but the only reason I got anywhere near close was that I went far out and built something unusual. People of my size 140 pounds wouldn't even think of going in speed trials. Laird Hamilton once told me he thought he was too light to go into speed trials and he is a serious beefer.

AC: Inner most limits on pure fun

GG: I am restoring that, to get it on the DVD. That is part of the computer battle I am having.

AC: Gee I hope the spoon comes back and the whole concept of having a flexible rocker, I mean no one really understood what you were doing there.

GG: the problem with that is, where are you going to use it in this day and age? They don't work unless you can draw the line you have to draw (like a formula one racing car) they don't work in crowded waves. I guess if you are big, and aggressive enough, you can go out there and get waves in the A grade spots.

AC: Have you ever worn a legrope?

GG: We used legropes in Tahiti, and in places like that. I've used them occasionally on the spoon

AC: How did you fix it to the spoon? (the tail of the spoon isn't more than a quarter of an inch thick)

GG: Fixed it to the front actually. The problem is that the tail of the spoon sinks, by putting it on the front (where it is more buoyant and streamlined) it comes back to you with no problem. I don't like the legrope dragging behind me either...so I used to use real thin bungy cord and put it under my shoulder and around my neck, so that if it tangled on the bottom, I could get it off. In Tahiti, it is really dangerous with your legrope getting tangled and then you drown. You get pitched there a lot. You can imagine trying to catch those waves on a spoon. Brocky had a piece of motorcycle inner tube around his ankle and he worked out how he could point his toes out and the tube would slip off.

GG: It's a shame that not many people will get to watch Dolphin Glide on the big screen, because the super 35mm quality and the post production kept all the quality of the original film...it didn't get lost through generations of post production.

GG: Echoes is timeless...and the same thing with 'coming of the dawn.' They will never date, because there is nothing in there to date it. It's not really possible to ride any deeper, I don't think it's possible, to ride any deeper in the tube, unless you use a model, you know? Unless you use a radio controlled model, or a lipstick camera on a pole and shoved it through the back of the wave on a jet ski.

AC: There would be 50 people dropping in on you if you were back that far anyway!

GG: That's the problem. You ride deep in the tube today, then you get dropped in on straight away.

George Greenough

"Shot on 'big as Texas' 35 mm film format Dolphin Glide is awesome, almost spiritual. The resolution is breathtaking."- "The making of Dolphin Glide is the best source of information available to those interested in George Greenough's methods and philosophy."

> Inside film

"I have surfed with dolphins many times. They are wild dolphins and come of their own free will. I surf on my own a lot... this is when most of the dolphin encounters while surfing happen. It is an incredible experience to look beside you while surfing in the curl, there is a dolphin looking at me less than an arm's length away... gliding in the wave's energy, not swimming. Coming out of the pocket, cutting back the dolphin moves right under me. Looking over the front of the mat, it's so close; I'm surprised it's fins aren't touching me. Turning off the bottom and cutting back, it matches my moves perfectly. Paddling back, a mother dolphin and baby join me, the baby dolphin riding the little bit of energy I'm creating with the bow wave of the mat. What do these sea creatures see and experience? That is what this film is about."

> George Greenough

"Dolphin Glide is something that I believe is going to keep on awakening the compassion for the dolphins and the ocean they live in being clean and the environment being safe for them and communications between dolphins and humans being explored. I have had some pretty cosmic experiences with dolphins... recently a dolphin saved my life."

> Dave Rastovich

"I was continually oohing and ahhing at the range of angles and perspectives that George was able to get. The images, shapes and motions he brought out on film were surreal, like some sort of lava lamp under the sea gone mad. There were times I thought someone had slipped something into the drink I had before the show, only to be grounded when the camera came above water for a brief glimpse of land."
> Santa Barbara Surfing

"It's a hypnotic trip below the waves to experience what we could never experience first-hand. Beautifully shot and constructed, it is a glimpse of the lives of dolphins that only an innovator like Greenough could capture."
> Melbourne International film festival

"Greenough has finished a project that transcends today's surf movie bubbles dramatically as he did over 30 years ago with his in-the-tube footage. This film goes beyond anything previously connected with surf films, to offer audiences an incredible experience shot from a dolphin's point of view.
> Mark Cherry Australian Art Review FCCA

"Nothing has changed around Greenough, people are still frothing to their friends about how amazing the guy is. Dolphin Glide is a profound statement in that it doesn't have any humans surfing, maybe that is because George hasn't seen any humans surfing that impresses him more than the timeless footage he shot with his first two surfing movies. Only George knows."
> AC

one. Terry Fitzgerald - Design. two. Wayne Burton - Nose ride. three. Neil Purchase.

As the founder of TRACKS magazine and the maker of the cult film 'Morning of the Earth', Albe has an iconic name in the surfing industry. What many don't know is that Albe's interests and passions extend far wider than ocean photography. Check the website for more details.

four. Baddy Treloar - Angourie. five. The late Bobby Brown - Angourie. six. Terry Fitzgerald - Kirra. seven. American expat Bob Cooper.

one. Frank Latta - Cult hero.

two. Col Smith - Kirra. three. Baddy Treloar - Angourie. four. Ted Spencer - Early highlines. five. Midget Farrelly - First World Champ. six. George Greenough - Freefall. seven. Lloyd Griffith - Crescent.

Photo: peterCRAWFORD

Photo's this story>
nigelANRNISON
mareaRYAN
andrewKIDMAN
lawrenceEASTLAND

Art of Farming

ART OF JAMMIN'

Jammin' is something many surfers are really into. Being in the groove while Jammin' is very similar to being in the groove with a wave, it is a rhythm, a feel, and it is a feel that some musicians live for, the art of Jammin'.

Surfing is an art form. You only have to watch a talented surfer riding the right board in the right waves/conditions, and you will feel it and witness the art form in motion: The surfboard becomes like an extension of the surfer's body and he/she is completely at one with the craft, the wave and themselves, and it is then that the artist begins to paint.

We have heard it all before that many surfers also like playing music, but what we delve into here is the unconscious side of surfing and music, the feeling of timelessness experienced with some art forms. With a current explosion in 'surfing music' and surfer musicians/artists, hopefully we are getting ready to experience the uncovering of more talented creative people that have a unique way of expressing themselves.

Some say the similarity (with surfing and music) is in the 'higher plane' that is often reached, a meditation-like zone that is only achievable if approached... as an art form. Asking a few surfers, who also play music, hopefully you can feel the tone of this story with the quotes and imagery...

"Writing about music is like dancing about architecture"
(Author unknown)

Art of Harmonix

Photos: AC

' music expresses that which cannot be said and on which it is impossible to be silent.' [anonymous]

Neal Purchase Jnr (Purcho): (Pioneer for free surfing and all round guitarist/musician/dad)

"Just listen…You get your break, when you're in a good jam, it's a great way to communicate with your friends on a different level like you wouldn't normally do and it brings people together. You

Jamie K: (Retired pro surfer and professional musician/artist/dad)

"The more you listen, the more toobed you get."

Shannon Sol R. Carroll: (Professional musician by night and tooob hound by day):

"For me the key similarity between surfing and jamming is the sense of timelessness you experience when you're fully immersed in the moment. When you're playing a melody or a solo you are like the surfer, drawing whichever lines the wave allows. The band can make a sonic wave jack up and barrel or fatten out into mush, double up and reel or just close out... It depends how well you're connected. Good sound connections usually make for good sound waves. The "jam barrels" happen when you're truly improvising your way into new territory and holding your respective lines as the track reels and throws."

Dave Rastovich (Rasta): (World class free surfer and percussionist/wombat)

"You know when you surf you catch a wave and then watch someone else catch a wave...there hasn't been one word communicated between the two of you but you know exactly how you're feeling you know...when you play music you can play a funky tune and get all funky, then get all mellow, then all funky again and stop and throughout not a word was spoken but you know exactly what the others are 'saying.'"

"They are so similar (surfing and jammin'), sometimes when you're jammin', like when you're surfing...one guy in the line-up sometimes tries to get more waves than the rest, he's frustrated and frothing, probably 'cos he's riding the wrong board (instrument?)..."

"Time is non existent when you're jammin'...a bit like surfing sometimes. The jamming thing is sharing... For me that's where it's at, the sharing thing. Some of the surfs I have had by myself have been amazing, but I know they would be far more enhanced/memorable if I had just one other person to share them with....a lot like jammin; you can belt out an epic tune on your own and go wow and it feels pretty good, but when there is someone else there tapping or strumming or singing along to that tune, it's even better...for me it feels great...it's cool because you're co creating...co-creating an epic vibe...together feeling the same thing without talking..."

Low Pressure Sound Systems

What happens when you get a dozen musicians, surfers, 4 camera people, a handful of creative women, a hero sound engineer, and put them all into a beach house for two weeks to go surfing and record music. Well, that is exactly what happened recently at a quiet coastal destination on the East coast of Australia. With no set 'plan' in place, the mission was to surf and record music and that is exactly what happened, but there was something more...there was some kind of intangible 'something' that can only be accounted for by the like mindedness and the sheer bassline of talent that was grooving to the rhythm and the stoke

The catalyst for this adventure was a core group of people (Low Pressure Sound Systems) who all have a similar ethos to the art of improvised fun, and this proved to set the platform for an amazing two weeks of infectious music by a group of musicians that are simply world class. Each night the music seemed to visit a different country and the versatile style of each musician added something unique to the mix. One minute the house would be quiet and laid back, with people working on computers and artworks, or taking a few photo's, or doing some interviews, or simply reading a book. Then someone would start tapping a drum, or a guitar...almost spontaneously another musician would pick up on the groove and a jam would begin, the sound guy would run out of his room and get the microphones spot on, then run back to his room to check the levels, almost like a wild animal hunting for prey. Within minutes there would be half a dozen musicians all grooving to some new beat, with the drums being held down tight by one *Terepai Richmond*, *James Cox* having a percussion set up fit for a jazz cat and the Bass lines were flowing free from *O.J Newcomb*, *Shannon Carroll was in*

the spotlight, playing some seriously fat guitar lines with vocals that James Brown would be happy with...it was funky in patches for sure, but then the mellow tones of *Dave Rastovich's* cosmic instruments, and *Chris Lane* with his flute playing added another ingredient to the recipe. It seemed that every day something different would happen, someone would hop on another instrument we hadn't heard them play before, or quite simply another musician or surfer would drop by and stay for a few days. One couldn't help but notice the stoke in the guys eyes playing together in an idyllic setting with waves crashing to the shore near by. The anticipation that more waves would be ridden in the morning, the serenity of having no mobile phones or emails to respond to, there was simply no pressure coming from anywhere...and that is when the artist really begins to paint.

The whole experience had a twist of the old school about it. I think any of our surfing forefathers would have been stoked to see us doing it again. We had a video projector beaming up material from

of the music. *George Greenough* gave us some material that he is working on for his new project 'behind the scenes' for us to come up with the sound, and it worked a treat. 'Coming of the dawn' was a highlight for me, hearing some serious drum and basse with that in-the-tube footage was a real buzz and Shannon Carroll just seems to put the right lines down on the guitar that actually transcends into the feeling we have while riding in the tube. What a treat. Thanks George.

Low Pressure Sound Systems is a collective of musicians/producers and sound engineers who record soundtracks and albums for surfing material. With a core band called 'the band of frequencies' headed by Shannon Carroll on guitar and vocals, this is something new and exciting for the surfing world. *Shannon Carroll* is a name that is new to surfing, or is it? Maybe it is Tom Carroll's cousin? Nah. Maybe his family has a long lineage of musicians that surf...well that is about the truth. 'Moonstone' was the band that entertained the Gold Coast surfers in the early 1970's, and many a story can be told of the old 'patch' days where Moonstone used to play every Wednesday to Saturday night! *'The Son of Moonstone,'* Shannon Carroll has several bands that he works with, and some of his recordings with the Neighbourhood Groove Collective and *Afrodizziact* can be heard on the switch-foot website. Shannon has developed a close relationship with Dave Rastovich (percussion) and together they are learning off each other in their passion for music and surfing. O.J (the juice) Newcomb holds down the basslines like a session musician should and the drums are held tight by the very likeable Terepai Richmond, who needs little introduction to anyone who knows drummers.

The two weeks wasn't all about surfing and music though, it was a lot to do with a gathering of like-minded people and at some stages it really felt like a tribe...with each individual having a place, a task and a feeling of togetherness, that while it might sound a bit fluffy... well, it was. It was a happy family, with dinner time being about the only time everyone slowed down to reflect and look forward.

Bali Strickland was in his element in and out of the water, he was truly bewildered by the talent of the musicians, and you could see the glee in his stride as he wandered the campus looking for the right angles. With over 40 hours of material to edit, he has his work cut out with the film...and with 50 hours of recorded music, there could be more than one album from 'the band of frequencies.'

There were cameras around and plenty of material was captured, to all be put into a DVD and at this stage no label has been put on it. The theme of the film will explore the peak experience of the surfer and the musician and attempt to identify with the apparent 'time warp, the 'no mind' phenomenon and the 'zone' that is felt in heightened moments while surfing and jamming or maybe even just reaching a level of focus that has no room for external noise... The entire sound track is a LP-Sound Systems production. Not much more needs to be said really...although one could write a book on it.

' music is your own experience, your thoughts, your wisdom.
if you don't live it, it won't come out of your horn. '
[charlie'BIRD'parker]

Jazz Funk n Blues

Ash Grunwald (Blues musician who tours to surf as much as he tours to gig):

"The 'Zone' that the surfer or musician experiences is a fleeting feeling at first, a moment where everything is in sync and a moment where time does indeed stand still, or perhaps just becomes irrelevant. This 'moment' becomes easier to access as skill level and experience make the practice second nature and the act of doing it is unconsciously derived rather than consciously thought out."

Lucas Proudfoot: (Retired pro surfer and leader of the band Max Judo)

"They are both a form of "self expression". There is no right or wrong way of expressing these two passions. Both surfing and music allow a person to show their style, whether it is a fast driving bottom turn on a nice 6ft day.... or a funky guitar riff on a lazy Sunday afternoon jam session. For me nothing tops off a day of great waves with ya mates than jamming the afternoon away with the sound of dueling guitars, soft bongo beats and the authentic sound of the didgeridoo. In the end no one is the best at surfing or the best at music it should all be fun and experimental..."

Terepai Richmond (session drummer and offshore reef explorer):

"3 degrees of jammin"

"Firstly...you need a passion for both art forms. Secondly... you need the skills to translate what your mind sees... into physical actions! Thirdly... open ears, mind and soul to act and react on the surroundings of your environment... be it, liquid medium of the ever changing oceans or the perpetual flow of a thick or thin audio experience!"

photo: simonWILLIAMS

Jazz / Funk n Blues

< Beau Young: (World champion surfer/wombat, and singer songwriter)

"I always refer to surfing like you're riding a horse, you're going with it unconsciously, but at the same time you're focused...you're unconsciously on a roll and at one with the horse you are riding and you are kind of trying not to think about the fact that you're moving pretty quick. I think jammin is the same in that you are with someone and you know consciously you don't want to go out of the jam...but unconsciously, the more unconscious you become the better you get at jammin...and I think surfing is exactly the same."

"I believe it's the same with people like Harry (Sketch Holiday) and their art you know. There is consciousness, but there is also the unconscious side...which I prefer to embark upon more than the conscious, because when you surf unconsciously and you jam unconsciously you're not adhering to any particular formula...you are just being...and that's what I think jammin is, it's an unconscious expression."

Jim Banks: (One of the original surfing explorers who also jams with his homemade guitars and valve amps)

"To me jamming is completely different from surfing, because surfing to me is a completely individual thing. The best surf I have is in the water by myself, just me and the ocean, whereas, with jamming it's a group of people interacting and allowing the music to come to life. The whole thing with jamming is it's about connecting with people intuitively and allowing the spontaneity to happen...in my favourite surf, there is spontaneity there also, but with the ocean. The pinnacle of Jammin' is the same as the pinnacle of surfing, it's being totally in the heart space. I find when the jam is really happening, it seems that none of my focus is actually on my own playing, it's on listening to everyone else and intuitively something comes out of my guitar that complements and dances with everyone else."

Andrew Kidman: (Surfing wombat, innovative movie maker and singer/songwriter)

"Jammin' is like surfing with friends. Sometimes you might be surfing with your friend and he is a better surfer than you and you will learn something right there...and it's the same with Jammin', you'll be sitting on the groove and you'll hear him do something and you'll let him go, because you want to hear him play... or watch him ride."

xavierRUDD: by mareaRYAN

'Every time I play, I get lost in a trance in a way. I open myself up and pour myself out and maybe people feel that and feel comfortable enough to do it themselves. Jamming is the most beautiful connection, when it's happening it all feels like one and it blows me away.'

xavier rudd

At switch-foot we are currently working on several soundtracks and independent albums with a stable of musicians that is world class. Check the website for more details, or to register your interest in this passion.

www.switch-foot.com

Peter Crawford's legacy lives on in the surfing world…if you spend a moment with Justin (his son) you can feel the influence not only within himself but also the little niche crew on the Northern beaches of Sydney. Justin is on the path to being a renowned surfing photographer himself and with mates like Brett Herring, they are pushing boundaries in board and fin design. PC's love and passion for fin design has been passed onto the next generation… that is important. PC's images represented here is a small section of his extensive library, a library that deserves to be open to the public, but a library that has largely gone astray until some honesty pulls up a chair at the table.

one. Point break. two. Bob Cooper.

two & three. Peter Crawford. four. George Greenough with camera. five. Cheyne Horan.

"I would still be a long lost drifter... no money, no direction, no body of work...if it wasn't for Mr Fate."

Sketch

• pipeline

American, Sketch Holiday, has been travelling in Australia since he was 21. Focusing on surfing art, his style is uniquely recognised wherever you see it. The following sketch holiday images are from a series of 11 works that have come from being deeply involved in the surfing subculture of the rainbow region (northern NSW) and spending time surfing with guys who display a style that stimulates this artistic flair. Sketch Holiday immersed himself in this subculture and he really helped to progress this movement in the artistic side of surfing.

Holiday

• two surfers

• tight walker

Sketch Holiday

"It all began a few years ago in Australia, I was just a goofy kid... rambling, drifting, floating, cruising, going with the flow or wherever my heart desired. I never dreamed of having my works documented/published in a magazine (or even in surfing films)... but Mr Fate he works in mysterious ways..."

"I was born in the middle of America but was on the move and travelling from the get-go, checking things out. A few years ago I wandered over to Australia and was beach bumming around... surfing and skating and hitch-hiking just cruising and having fun... spending most of my days on the beautiful beaches surfing and filling up sketch book after sketch book with drawings and writings. Then one day I met another Californian transplant disillusioned with the whole scene back home and his name was Harry Daily and he was another artist and he had one of my sketchbooks (with him) and he said he had been on my trail for weeks!"

"I left the sketch book in a phone booth for this girl to come and find me and follow me up the coast and have romantic adventures with me, but I guess he found it and he followed it instead, because he liked the drawings and writings inside."

"Harry was a Californian artist travelling the east of Oz looking for adventure and excitement and we met up and made a good team; he helped me with my art and I introduced him to girls and such. He loved my drawings so much and he was a natural teacher with many tricks up his sleeves...and he showed me everything...and I hope in a way he could say the same about me."

"So I started painting and working with him, I loved it, I took to it swimmingly and I learned to paint and was painting well in no time at all. Harry was very inspiring and helpful."

"So the paintings in this book are a medium size series I did in water colour at the end of my study. I was heavily inspired by Harry Daily, Andy Davis and Art Noveau."

• 2 ninnies

" when the spirit does not work with the hand, there is no art." [leonardoDAvinci]

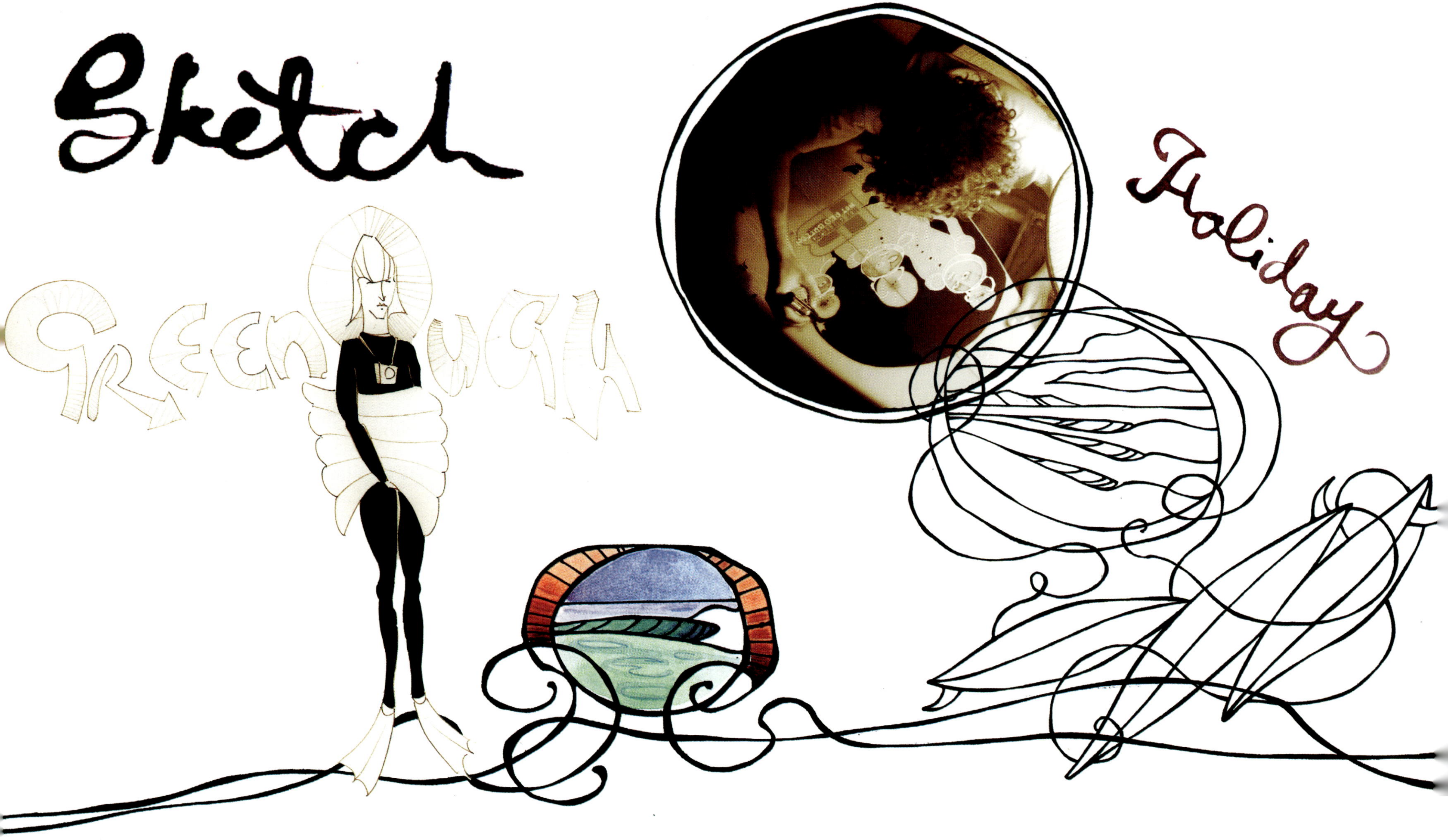
Sketch
Holiday
GREEN

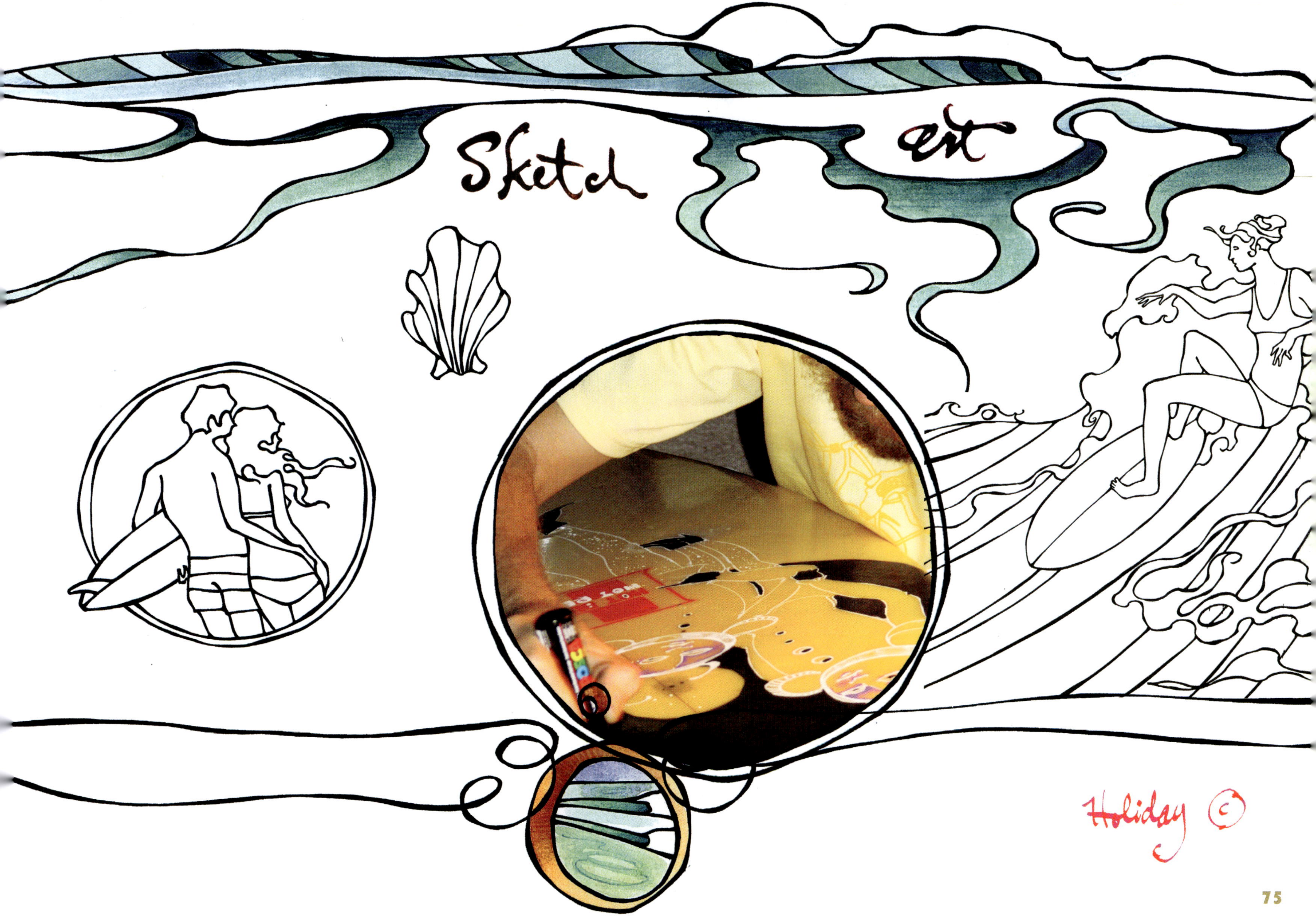
Sketch it
Holiday ©

• dream surf

" art is the most intense mode of individualism that the world has known." [oscarWILDE]

Is Sketch a surfer?

• Yeah. He started surfing a few years ago back in America and then picked it up more over here in Australia. He more just liked to do everything and was really good at whatever he picked up.

Does Sketch still surf?

• Yeah of course, loves surfing.

Does Harry still surf?

• Not that much anymore

Why doesn't Harry surf anymore?

• I dunno, why doesn't Harry surf anymore...he doesn't find it fulfilling anymore, nobody seems to be having a good time out there, everyone's grumpy, people like to crash into him...he's out of tune, he's overweight.

Is it because people heckle?

• Yeah probably

What sort of stuff do they yell out in the surf?

• The best is when I surfed past these young kids and then they totally mimicked my style to each other doing hand gestures and stuff to each other....that was a low blow, mocking me like that. hahaha.

• AC •

Sketch Holiday

These prints are for sale on the website, check it out. www.switch-foot.com

• adam & eve

one. Wayne Lynch with Rip Curl Quiver. two. Rip Curl's Claw. three. Keith Paull - Bells 1974. four. Dick Harvey.

Steve Cooney is famous for exploring Uluwatu as a bright-eyed teenager in the early 1970's in the classic surf film Morning of the Earth. What many people don't know is that he was also around to take some classic shots of some of surfings 1970's icons. This is a small representation of Steve's library and further images can be viewed on the website.

five. Rabbit at DVS factory 1974. six. Simon Anderson - Single fin soul - Nth Narrabeen 1975. seven. MP Fangtail - Pa Bendell 1974. eight. Wayne Lynch with Rip Curl Quiver.

GLASS LOVE

Andrew Kidman: "In the film I wanted to feature the generational link and love of surfing that gets passed down through families, in particular through the Curren and Purchase families. The sons are surfers and their fathers are surfer/shapers. It was nice to peer in on a small part of their relationship and how surfing makes them special. This factor, and the continued experimentation with board design, was the highlight for me in making the film."

" not everything that can be counted counts, and not everything that counts can be counted." [albertEINSTEIN]

THE VAL DUSTY EXPERIMENT PRESENTS
LITMUS
©1996
A SURFING ODYSSEY
TO ENTER THE KINGDOM OF HEAVEN ONE MUST BE CHILDLIKE
Derek Hynd
Tom Curren
John Francis Dargo
Joel Fitz
Wayne Lynch
Leonard Mar
MUSIC BY THE VAL DUSTY EXPERIMENT and The Screaming Orphans
ALSO FEATURING
dream
- FILMED IN 65mm WANKAVISION -
- ART BY BROWN - SUTHO - KIDMAN -

The sun goes down on a relatively unexploited right hand sand-bottom point somewhere south of the Gold Coast. A few surfers trade the dying end of a glassy two to three feet of swell. Peaks feather, bend, and run at warp speed down the bank. You can see Andrew's travelling in his surfing, the way he never seems to be racing, his unassuming calm. As a subject for interview Kidman is fascinating. His artistic accomplishments alone are staggering. He has been at times a magazine editor, filmmaker, photographer, artist, musician and journalist. More importantly, he has retained his independence in both character and perspective throughout. Eventual dissatisfaction with the magazine industry, and interest in alternative forms of media resulted in an intense year of global travel and the creation of 'Litmus – a surfing odyssey.' Glass Love, the long awaited second film from Andrew, reinvestigates the magic of the surfing world that he attempted to portray nearly a decade before, in Litmus. This, however, is a solo outing, without the val dusty experiment on board, and the nature of the film reflects this.

Litmus was the classic story of an underground film that many people initially dismissed and subsequently embraced and praised. Released at a time when the corporations and the corporate branding of surfing were really establishing a foothold in collective consciousness, and surf travel was incessantly marketed as a solely tropical adventure, Litmus was a radically different take on the situation.

Primarily focusing on cold-water destinations; an unusual but breathtakingly talented variety of surfers were shown performing in their chosen environments. The environment in the early nineties was changing dramatically. Slater and the generation of rippers who accompanied him were changing the face of surfing. Professionalism was becoming big business, idols were being born, and (in some peoples' opinion) the narrow focus of competitive surfing was gathering momentum.

'That's why we (Jon Frank, Mark Sutherland and Andrew Kidman) made Litmus, just for people to enjoy surfing, just to go; 'surfing is still great, and don't worry about that other stuff.'

Performance boundaries were being blown apart during this period, but it is conceivable that other aspects of surfing were suffering.

'The stuff those guys are doing is phenomenal... it's amazing. The places those high performance guys are taking surfing is just mind blowing. But you can either be a part of it, or you can't be a part of it and we just didn't want to be a part of it. And we knew there were a whole lot of other people out there who weren't a part of it, and that's maybe why Litmus struck a chord with people.''

It is now ten years since Litmus was released...do you think it has been the indicator for change and if so what changes have occurred in the surfing industry since then?

"It's funny you should say that, because we were going to call the movie 'change.' A mate of ours down in Victoria, Russell Graham, he had a surfboard company back in the day called 'change'. Litmus is like a metaphor for change, you know, with the Litmus test and that. (Russell Graham is a full-blown legend, he has the best collection of boards you have seen and he isn't selling them. I hope you print that). I don't think Litmus really made any changes...I mean maybe people saw it and became liberated to know that they could ride whatever they wanted and it didn't matter? I think Derek's surfing at J-Bay made the fish design 'available' to people... even Tom Curren you know."

Artwork by: harryDAILY

Both Litmus and Glass Love feature music by Andrew and friends. A talented guitarist and vocalist, Andrew's solo album, The Spaces in Between, is a work of sincere expression. He laughs as he describes his musical evolution from three chords up:

'When I was doing that album, it was like, you have to learn the fundamental process of the blues, before you can go away and do something creative with it. You got to learn something before you break it apart. Picasso had to learn how to paint before he could attempt cubism. The album was a lot about that. Then there are other sides to that album too. I did know what music I wanted to play. I think you hear that on the album.'

' only constant repetition will finally succeed in imprinting an idea on the memory of the crowd.'

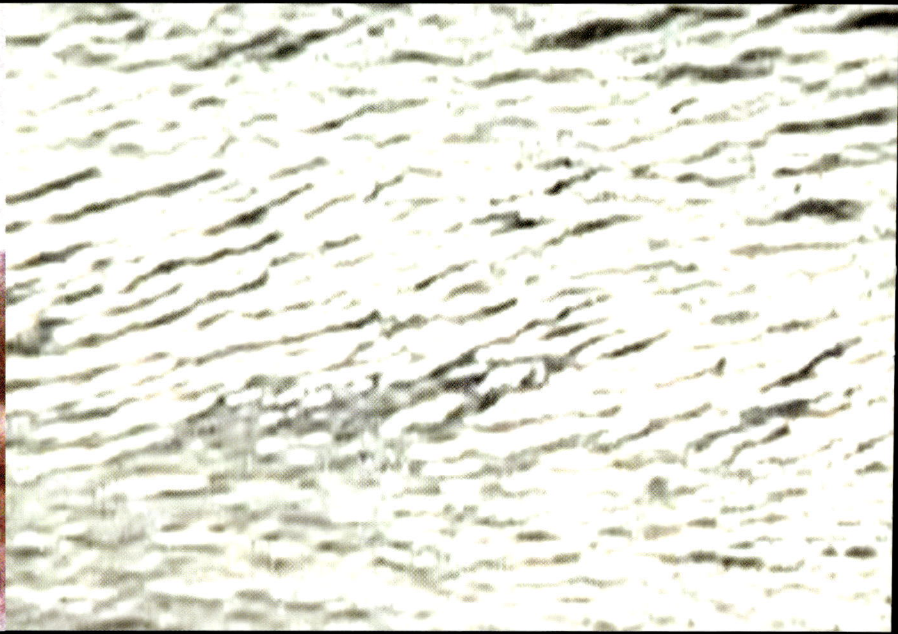

Derek is a subject close to Andrew's heart. A phenomenal surfer foremost, and a global seedling for open-minded stoke second. Andrew's eyes glint when he talks about Derek's surfing:

'He surfs better now than he ever has. It's funny because when people see Litmus, they think, fuck, Derek Hynd rips... He knows what he wants to do, he knows how he wants to surf, I think that's an important thing...to know your limitations of what you can and can't do. I'd love to see him after a consistent swell...after he was honed in.'

Derek's surfing, although seemingly flamboyant, is actually calculated and functional. Whilst his movement on waves will aesthetically appeal to only some surfers, it is inconceivable to say that the boards don't work...and this was ten years ago. A previous trip to J-bay had proved inspirational and thought provoking.

'I used to go and stay with him, and he had the quiver when I first went. We were riding 18 ¼ 'banana boards', and that was our quiver to take on Jeffrey's Bay! You get to Derek's house and he had 30 surfboards, each and every one was a different board. Almost the reason he wanted you there, I don't think it was pre-meditated or anything. One of the things I think he enjoyed about you being there was riding his boards. He was stoked to let you go out on those boards. The more you rode those boards, the more you realised how onto it he was. That was when I asked him, and told him I was going to leave the magazines.'

Why?

'I was just over it. Going from experiencing that in surfing, and spending time with Wayne, you are just over it, you don't want to do it. You see the way those people are living and how much enjoyment they are getting out of whatever they are doing, and you think I could be doing that too, in some other way. I asked them, could we show you riding that stuff?'

Thankfully for surfing as an activity the response was yes.

'They didn't mind us showing other people that. Someone like Derek definitely knew that having a quiver had enriched his surfing. Derek is the sort of person who wants to share that with everybody, he always has been. For us to go and capture it and show it on a wider scale, like with the film... he was stoked, not an ego thing at all, just to get other people stoked.'

Andrew sacrificed a hell of a lot to create Litmus:

'It changed my life. I was back in Sydney, I didn't have a job, I didn't have anything, I was broke. I was living in a garage...You think you've gone out and done something important, and you are broker than you ever have been, you've got less work than you ever have done, and no one really cares. It's funny, people seem to care about Litmus now, but at the time no one could care less. They thought it was shithouse. It came out at a time when no one was really looking at that aspect of surfing.'

"It changes your life, everything changes your life."
Andrew Kidman

Along with seeing inspiring images of his old man's surfing style and watching old surfing movies, Neal Purchase Jnr was inspired to start experimenting with different boards through seeing Derek Hynd's surfing in Litmus. This was one of Andrew's principal desires in revisiting filmmaking, to investigate the repercussions of Litmus. Luckily for Neal, his father (Neal Snr.) enjoys his son's new direction, and is happy to provide the boards for Neal to experiment with (although it did take much convincing) and Neal has totally put his own interpretation into riding these boards; Andrew is full of interest in Neal's surfing:

'He's great, he's a great surfer... he's kind of old school in a lot of ways because he does take a line. You either do or you don't in surfing. A lot of guys break the line, and when you break the line you lose speed. I think that's one thing Neal has always done... he's always held a line through his surfing. As soon as you get on these different kinds of boards that hold lines better... that are better when they hold a line... that's when you start seeing some interesting surfing, especially in a backhand situation.'

"I just wanted to show something that's unique. We all know Neal is a good surfer, but I wanted to show how the surfboards worked, through how good Neal surfed. It was interesting because it was like the Derek Hynd story (Litmus) with all those boards and now this is like the next step...this is how good they work, through a surfer like Neal Purchase Jnr. Where Neal takes it is a whole new area for surfboard design, because Derek was definitely riding old 70's single fins. It took a long time to find someone like Neal, because everyone else seems to be riding these boards for a different reason...Neal was unique and doing it anyway."

"Neal is lucky because his father is so ahead of the game. It's completely cutting edge. There is a difference between retro and cutting edge. Re-making something from the past is fun, but doesn't mean you are going to be able to go into the future with your boards. All this modern technology that has been developed over the last thirty years with the rails, you apply that with, say, the thickness from the 70's boards, then you apply the new fin set ups that you can get going with the rockers and everything that they've learnt about concaves and you're going to have a board like what Neal's father is making, or like what Parmenter or Wayne Lynch makes."

Shaper: patCURREN

Glass Love also features Tom Curren and his brother Joe and the relationship they have with surfer/shaper/father Pat. This is another of the messages that arise through Litmus and Glass Love; the idea of surfing as a maturing sport. To observe two generations of Currens, perhaps one of the greatest families in modern surfing history, is undeniably an incredible experience. The shaping process and the riding process are all documented and suffice to say, the board is a gem. Andrew is once again animated when he describes Pat...

'Curren was interesting because I wanted to see Pat shape a board, personally...I didn't care if I filmed it, I just wanted to see it. Of course he's going to do it differently! I just wanted to see it, I've seen everybody else shaping, and I wanted to see him do it. Just for my own...I love that stuff, I love watching people shape boards...it's a fascinating thing, it's like watching someone paint a picture...'

That's the thing with Pat or Simon Anderson, Dave Parmenter, Dain, they are all unique, and they want to pass it on. They want people to see...this is how you sharpen a tool... because they know what it does for them. That's how people learn to shape, they watch other people shape. That's how Dain knows how to shape, from watching Bob shape the whole time, and a load of other people. I know how to shape because I've watched Simon shape, or I've watched Parmenter shape. That's the only way you ever know.'

Surfer: andrewKIDMAN

Kidman: "I am just trying to blend ALL the good stuff into one board. Even asymmetric subtleties you know."

Would you say that Glass Love focuses further on the artistic side of surfing?

Kidman: "Nah...it's focused on a lot of other stuff too. It's not just artistic... It's design, it is life. I was looking for characters that were purely interested in experimenting with surfboards, and the struggles that they undergo. It's the struggle that is the story I think."

You are not well known for your surfing or your passion for surfboard design and functionality...yet at the cutting edge of surfing Beau Young, Purcho and Rasta all give you credit for how you have helped them...how have you managed to stay out of the spotlight for your surfing?

Kidman: "I don't care mate. I just enjoy surfing... if I can. Being a good surfer puts you in places that are unbelievable. George would say the same thing, he is an unbelievable surfer and he is happy with being a good surfer because he gets to be in places in nature that are unbelievable. It's good to be a competent surfer. That's all I'd say."

It seems that you have largely done the entire project by yourself, from organising and sourcing the footage/vision, to editing, to the soundtrack to the distribution...how important is it for you to your creative independence throughout and do you think this 'formula'/method helps in the artistic direction?

Kidman: "Well...the reason I do it myself...it's the only way financially that I can do it. Nobody is coming to me saying 'we'll give you all this money' but you know I think that taints it in some way too. ... I'm happy to be independent. In making a film you work with a lot of other people (Neal, Joe and Tom Curren), so it's not really independent. All the people in the film have done a lot of work to help make the film, it's not all me you know. I put it together. I'm just trying to represent them and who they are anyway."

Have you put it all on the line again with Glass Love like you did with Litmus and how has it been trying to balance the work load and the new family life with your first child Bella?

Kidman: "You put it all on the line with everything you do. I think. I do anyway, because I don't have a choice. Anyone that is going to put something out there, whether they want to paint a picture, write a song...if you are presenting something physical to the world, you are putting it all on the line. It's not safe. There is a lot of bullshit art out there; you can believe whatever you want really."

After spending a bit of time with Andrew you get the impression that if it weren't for all the other things he has wound up doing, he would love to be at work in a shaping bay, putting out functional and unique boards. Something that Andrew and Neal still share is eternal grommethood, they are stoked on waves, stoked on the beauty surrounding them, stoked on life.

one. Wayne Dean - Kirra. two. Michael Peterson - Stubbies 1977. three. Skate USA. four. Lennox Head. five. Peter Drouyn, John Mantle, Kieth Paull, Randy Rarrick, Carmel - Hawaii. six. Mark Richards.

Dick Hoole doesn't need an introduction to anyone who knows surfing, even the Queen of England has recognized his services to the sport. A photographer, a film-maker, a distributor, an entrepreneur and an all round good bloke. More of Dick's work can be accessed at the website and check out the story on his famous surfing film Storm Riders which is now available on DVD

seven. Skate USA. eight. Unknown - Soul Arch. nine. Michael Peterson. ten. Michael Peterson.

HOW TO MAKE THE CLASSIC SURFING ADVENTURE FILM

1 *In theory anyone could make the classic surfing adventure film. Here's how: First of all gain the support and participation of the cream of todays best surfers. Not just the worlds top professional competitors, but also those adventurous surfers who will do anything and go anywhere for an uncrowded wave. Like Wayne Lynch, Peter McCabe, Gerry Lopez, Thornton Fallander, Tommy Carroll, Joe Engel, Simon Anderson, Mark Richards, Rabbit Bartholomew, and a supporting cast of dozens.*

2 *Make sure your credit cards are paid up so you can get out there for two years and cover over 70 different locations on five continents — not only travelling the well trodden path to popular spots, but also off the beaten track to the most exotic and exciting undiscovered spots left on earth. Like Malaysia, Sumatra, Java, Bali, Africa, Hawaii, The Great Australian Bight, Big Bells, Sydney, Newcastle, Gold Coast, plus new locations that have never before been seen on film.*

3 *Fly back to Australia and go to Victoria for the largest gathering of windsurfing champions ever. Then fly off to Hawaii where the pioneers of the surfboards with sails will dazzle you with airborne acrobatics in the huge Hawaiian surf. Like Robbie Naish, Cort Larned, Mike Waltze, Mark Paul and Mike McGuire at Johanna Beach and Hookipa Park on Maui.*

4 *Next it comes to music, and you have to have lots of that. Go out and buy over 400 record albums of the best Australian music available. Take it all home and listen to over 4800 tracks until your ears bleed, narrowing it down to 35 of the best songs. Like Australian Crawl, Split Enz, Mondo Rock, Little River Band, Men At Work, The Church, Sharon O'Neill, Moving Pictures, Matt Finish, Jo Jo Zep, Radiators, Mi Sex, Mark Gillespie, Models, Hunters and Collectors, Joey Harris, Steve Powell and many more.*

It's not easy, and in theory you could go out and produce all of the above. However, may we suggest that you simply leave it to us and come along and see our latest film, "STORM RIDERS

STORM RIDERS are young and free and ready for anything! Travel with them to 5 continents to discover the exotic jungles of Sumatra, Java, romantic Bali and the blistering desert Outback of Australia. Ride the treacherous coastlines of Africa and the Great Australian Bight. See men and women pit their courage against the biggest waves ever filmed, share wilderness waves with wild dolphins, and Windsurf on huge life-and-death waves in Hawaii. These are the STORM RIDERS, and they are going to take you on the ride of your life. Simply the greatest ocean adventure ever filmed!

'Stormriders' is now available on DVD from www.switch-foot.com

Photo: dickHOOLE

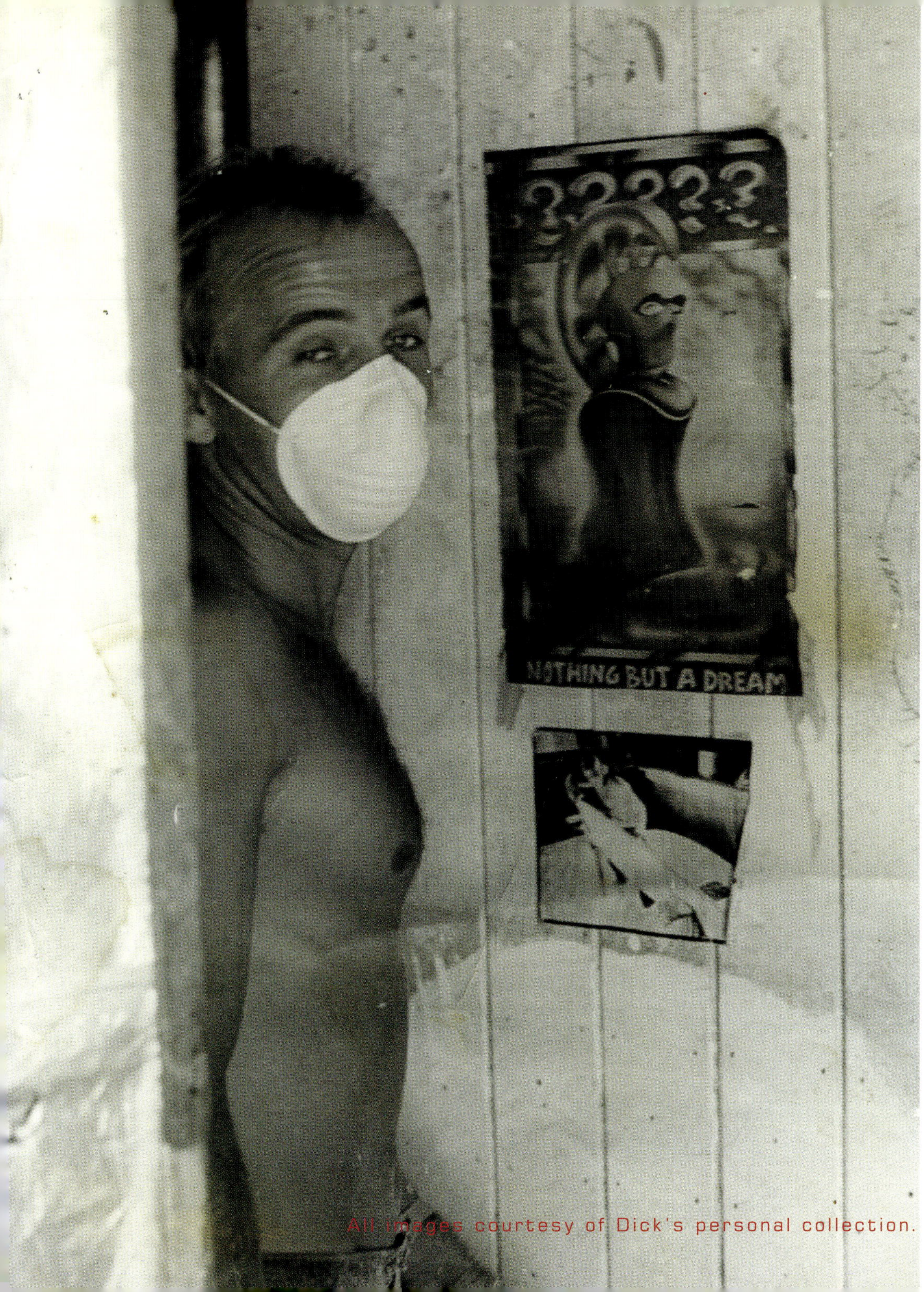

All images courtesy of Dick's personal collection.

DICK VAN STRAALEN
THE FLYING DUTCHMAN

love balance awareness freedom

What a great time to talk to Dick Van Straalen (DVS), one of the world leaders in surfboard innovation, and, a classic waterman. While DVS may today be famous for shaping interesting boards for one *David Rastovich (Rasta)* you will read throughout this article that DVS is an innovator and always has been. Now that this whole concept of riding interesting boards is almost 'fashionable,' DVS is no longer alone in his quest for experimentation. With an underground cult following for more than 30 years you will also notice that Van Straalen is one of the ten legends of Australian surfing that is featured in our benchmark story, the Tribal Elders. Alongside names such as Mark Richards, Nat Young and George Greenough you begin to understand that Van Straalen is more than a shaper. Van Straalen is a pioneer for sustainable surfboard manufacturing, the operator of the first Australian surfing school, the inventor of the 'Coolite' surfcraft, a great surfer, a family man, a philosopher and a huge contributor to the development of surfing in Australia and around the globe.

"I'm contributing to the 85% of surfing that everyone seems to forget about. There is a little minority over here that everything is focused on and I am way over here on the other side of surfing that no-one gives a shit about."

photo courtesy of Albe Falzon

Van Straalen was one of the first Sydney surfers who moved to Queensland. Shortly after he got married in Sydney he thought he better get a job that paid money, so he started working with Qantas Airlines. A perk of this job was regular 2-3 week holidays and this is when he would get in the Kombi bus and travel north to Queensland. 'Then we wanted to get away from parental pressure and thought, why not move to Queensland? At the time there was a whole group of us, there was like 20 of us living in this house. Then out at the farm I started working for Ken Goodnsvager who had just opened Adler Surf in Brisbane...he gave me a car and I was shaping boards on the farm and driving them up to Brisbane to finish and polish them...then we saw a vacant shop in Kirra and I said why don't we start a shop at Kirra called Spirit of the Sea and he said no worries...and we opened Spirit of the Sea...we also started a factory down the road to make the boards...there was myself, Keith Paul, Rick Neilsen and I think Neal Purchase shaped a few...we were making all the boards that went into Brisbane and the Spirit of the Sea shop at Kirra. The Old Burleigh theatre arcade was shortly after 1970...a lot of changes in that period were due to drugs...it all just changed you know. We opened the factory on the highway and when that burnt down it all kind of went in a different direction and changed again with Sea Island clothing and me shaping underground. When the clothing thing started to wind up I met Dave (Rasta) in about 1995 and that got me into shaping again and here we are now.'

Van Straalen will tell you that surfboard innovation has been suppressed by the industry and the media that is all ruled by a central myopic reality with too much focus on the competitive side of surfing, and not enough focus on the dream, the artistic realms of surfing and surfing history. Van Straalen talks about seeing people walking down the street with their 'surf' shirts on...people that don't even surf. 'Surfing does NOT have it's own statement anymore.' He talks about the loss of individualism within surfing and how 'back in the day' surfing was a pool of individuals all with a common thread, all with a common interest and that was, living the dream.

'It's the nature of the sport. In the early days with surfing, there was no fence around it. As contest surfing grew, they put a fence around it, and said, you can't go outside this fence, because we don't know how to judge it. We don't know how to evaluate when you step outside it. Everyone went and hopped inside that box. Now everyone is going; I'm sick of being in this pen, and now I'm going to step outside. Just in the last six months, I can't believe the change.'

Van Straalen is a positive and intelligent man. He has been there from the beginning of this surfing boom...he has seen mates go from living in a Kombi van to being multi-millionaire surfing industry tycoons...he has also seen mates go the other direction. The mainstream still contains some basic ironies for Van Straalen, not least the division between the art of shaping and the rest of the industry.

"When surfing started, surfboard manufacturers were the only people who advertised in surfing magazines. Now, surfboard manufacturers can't afford to advertise in surfing magazines. Without us, there is no surfing industry, there isn't, full stop, no argument. They are all riding on our backs. We are the horses and they are the jockeys. They don't help the surfboard industry whatsoever.' Van Straalen never conformed to the 'box' that is competitive surfing; he kept shaping boards for functionality and still does today. Anyone who knows Dick knows that he is an artist...an artist living the dream. Living the dream back in the late 1960's and still living the dream today shaping boards, surfing and all with his family...the family unit he views as the most important element to it all.

"I've been lucky in my life as far as the sort of surfers we've attracted, but that again, it's most probably the way we think and what we are putting out we attract, and we have attracted kids that are responsive to what we are doing. I'm lucky that I have dealt with people like Dave (Rasta) and Thornton Fallander, Joe Engel, Michael Ho and Mark Foo and everyone else you know...because they all help you and we are all helping each other grow, which I find is really satisfying... and all of this...most of it wouldn't be possible without meeting my partner in life Ann, and my kids... because that's basically why I did it...because we're a family and I had to provide for my family and my wife supported me the whole time through it...that's a big part of it...we've been married 38 years. It's a family thing and being a dad, which is really important to me."

"When we first started doing this I didn't want any of this...I just wanted the dream, the lifestyle, the tribal component where we are like a family and everyone looks out for each other...you know today people calling me a guru, I didn't want to be known as a guru, I'm just a person having a go...there is nothing enlightening about what we are doing.... just we are having a go and we have a different view and opinion of what's going on...and basically we are looking more at the artistic side of it than the competitive side of it...and I think surfing should have been an artistic form rather than a competitive form...but then you had people who wanted it to be competitive."

surfing world
AUSTRALIA'S SURFING MONTHLY
Registered at the General Post Office, Sydney, for transmission by post as a Periodical.
Vol.7 No.1 NOVEMBER 1965 PRICE: FOUR SHILLINGS
WINDANSEA SUCCESS STORY
THE NEWCASTLE AND SOUTH COAST CHAMPIONSHIPS · DOC SPENCE PROFILE · PHOTO STORIES ON WOONONA AND LENNOX HEAD · THE NEGLECTED SURFING SNEATS · THE PERFECT WAVE

The right wing of the Surf Company
is extremely industrious

On the road out of Burleigh Heads, going due west, you come across a sprawling industrial estate. On the right hand side of the road, huge exhibition surfing stores cover apartment block spaces; multiple tonnes of surf produce. Nestled neatly into the industrial estate, on the other side of the road, is a small factory containing a man of seemingly inexhaustible energy. A sharper contrast couldn't be more evident. Dick Van Straalen is a master shaper, the epitome of a committed long-term devotee to his craft. Dick was at Burleigh in the late 1960's and he is still there today and still shaping a huge variety of surf craft from old balsa Malibu's to single fins, to quad fins to paddle boards...he has a well balanced take on the concept of the quiver unlike many surfers and even shapers in the modern era.

But Dick hasn't been churning out surfboards for all those years, as fate dictated the script along another path. In the early 1980's his business literally burned to the ground, taking templates and rocker curves with it which changed Dick's direction entirely leading him into the clothing business with wife Ann and good mate Johnny Charlton (JC).

The early 1980's was the era of Simon Anderson's thruster and Dick welcomed the break from full time shaping. He kept shaping boards underground and kept his finger on the pulse with post-modern design ideas. It has only been the recent relationship developed with Dave Rastovich that has inspired him to get into it full scale again and he can't believe how much he is enjoying it and also how much people love his products. One product that is proving really popular is his Styrofoam fish; a model no doubt made more popular by Rasta's radical style on the craft, not to mention the renaissance of the Skip Frye/Steve Lis inspired kneeboards that people are standing up on these days...a shape that was invented back in 1965...taking 40 years to be accepted by the mainstream.

'I just like the variety of what we are attacking. I'd say it's like an artist. I don't consider myself as a shaper; I'm just basically a vibration shaper. I don't go too much into measurements; I'm not worried about how wide it is here, or how thick it is there. It's basically a feeling that you get."

Blaze sparks Dick's hopes

Top Coast surfboard manufacturer Dick Van Straalen with the remains of some of the boards destroyed by fire. The $15,000 blaze has Dick even more determined to succeed in his business.

Board maker will shape up again

DICK Van Straalen, one of the Gold Coast's leading surfboard manufacturers, joked with friends yesterday as he sifted through the charred remains of his uninsured, fire gutted factory.

The $15,000 fire which completely destroyed the business Dick built up over the last 12 years has made him even more determined to succeed.

Destroyed

"I'm going to have a holiday and then come back and start again," said the bronzed board builder whose customers include many of the world's great board riders.

For Van Straalen the fire — believed to have started with an electrical fault at 11.07 pm on Tuesday — is a major setback. Neither the factory, in Hibiscus Haven, Miami, nor its contents were insured.

Dozens of new surfboards, including some just built for Coast surfers Joe Engel and Thornton Fallander to take to competitions in Victoria, were destroyed.

Dick said: "Because of the structure of the factory and the amount of inflammable chemicals stored here, it was impossible to insure it." He said it was amazing that resin and chemicals stored in the factory did not explode.

Dick Van Straalen surfboards are sold throughout Australia and Dick has a reputation overseas for surfboard manufacturing.

So while the fire has been a major setback, Dick says he is in a better position to start again than when he first started.

"At least we are not starting with nothing," he said.

Three fire units went to the blaze on Tuesday night, but the factory was gutted within 10 minutes.

Firemen estimate damage at $17,000 — $15,000 worth of contents and $2000 damage to the small factory.

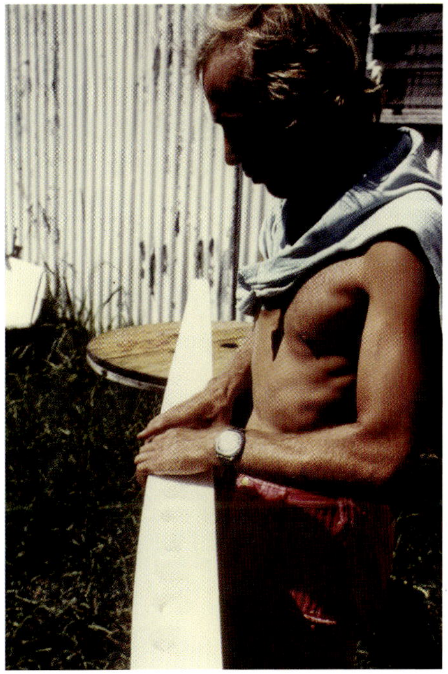

THE SURF COMPANY BURLEIGH HEADS QLD.

Dick's surfer/shaper friendship with *Dave Rastovich* has been widely publicised, and it seems to be a perfect symbiotic relationship. Dick speaks of Rasta with obvious affection; *"we clicked from day one. I've helped him, and he's helped me. It's a two way street. The other day he said to me; this just seems to be getting better and better. We are clicking more and more and understanding exactly what's going on. The best thing about it is, there is no limit to what we can do."* It is a relationship that was destined, one is a master shaper and finely tuned into the whole spectrum of surfcraft, and the other, a world class surfer who loves riding experimental boards and together they are making huge changes in the surfing world.

How instrumental has Dick been for your development in surfing?

• I met Dick when my parents split up, and I started hanging around with Dick a fair bit, and just being a grommet around his shaping bay. Being that surfing can be a reflection of your personality, Dick was affecting my personality by being completely open minded and judgeless."

How stoked are you to have arguably the most innovative shaper of our history shaping you any board you desire?

• Oh it's amazing. We are good friends. When we are hanging out and talking about boards and waves and life in general we are both just kids. Dick is an artist, he isn't a mathematical man, it's a real art form with Dick, and he doesn't use numbers and things he just does what he feels and what comes to his hands. There is never any repetition with shapes; he is always working on something new. In ten years I have never had a board that's even close to one I've had shaped before. Now we really know each other really well and he knows how far I can go with experimental boards. The funny thing with Dick is that I have never had a board off him that doesn't tube-ride well."

You just shaped a board yourself, what was the inspiration for that?

•It goes... It flies! I rode a Skip Frye of similar length and I knew it would take me a long time to get a board like that off Skip, so I thought screw it, I'll shape it myself. It's pretty simple and I knew what I wanted you know with the length and the rails and the thickness so I had a go. I shaped it at Jim Banks outdoor shaping bay.

What style of surfcraft is really exciting you right now?

• Just tweaking fish designs with radical concaves. The last board Dick shaped me he wrote on the bottom something old, something NEW. Basically that's all it is, he is using templates from 30 years ago. Any boards over 6'10 and I am riding a standard thruster set-up. Anything under 6"8' is pretty colourful and pretty whacked out.

Van Straalen: *"The fish is good because we are taking a different angle on it with Styrofoam™. The pocket rocket is really good because it is helping a lot of recreational surfers enjoy their surfing more. I just like making everything and having Dave at the high performance end of the scale really helps with the diversity. It's coming back. Everything has it's place in what we are doing. Simmons had three fins*

Rasta, riding a stringerless four foot ten surf craft, that was shaped from the scooped out dish of a paddle board.

Photos: andrewKIDMAN

"I don't think there is such a thing as a bad board just a bad choice of equipment on the day."

on a board in the forties. The biggest thing I hate about surfing is someone saying; I invented this. We are just a part of a chain. I'm just carrying the ball because someone has passed it to me, I'm carrying it and then I'll pass it to someone else. Without what's gone on before us we wouldn't be where we are right now. It's part of a progression we are going through."

With the rise in mainstream acceptance of experimental Surf-craft and particularly boards that trim well...what effect do you hope this will have on the general mindset of surfers in the water?

• All my aspirations are for the line-up is that people stop caring what they look like and just have fun. If it's a sleek board that makes them have fun, then good for them...if it's a longboard, then good for them...if it's an air matt, then good for them...any old thing as long as they are having fun everything else will work itself out...all the aggression will fade away.

We talked about the two sides of surfing, competitive and fun. Are you excited about the rise of 'the other side of surfing'? What can we do to nourish this movement? Or is it just a "fad" as being described by some media types?

• I see a difference between the retro fad and people doing what they feel. I feel there is a fad with the retro movement, but what I am part of (with this whole subculture and friends) is just pure joy and an internal joy, not a pre-packaged marketed idea of retro joy or future joy or soul or whatever you want to call it. We all have a choice between love and fear.

What can you say about the retro revival?

• I'm part of a seedling of a culture that's happening right now that includes you, that includes Kidman, Thomas Campbell, The Malloy's, Harry, Neal Purchase...there are so many people that are all part of this core group of people who are bringing the surfing pendulum back from the mostly materialistic view, the every man for himself point of view...it's bringing the pendulum back and not bringing right back to the other side like the 1960's which was far out and really loose, but bringing it to the middle where you have a professional act (like your book or Neal's clothing line), but not only doing that professional side but bringing in some elements from the other side; the looseness, the creativity, the experimentalism, the free thinking and being uncontrolled by external forces...bringing all that left field looseness to the middle as well to marry the creativity with the professional side to create something that is totally new...it has never happened before...it is very new and it is very exciting.

How do you feel about being a role model for kids?

• All these grommets are looking out for some kind of blueprint for how they should grow up and how they should act and whatever else you know...and the surf companies put those characters out there as role models, and I am just one of those characters. I am fortunate enough that I don't have to stick to a mould, to be one of those characters.

What are some of the key philosophies you have gathered from your spiritual search; particularly with eastern thinking/religion/lifestyle?

• Just balance really. The heart to, opening up your heart and having a really clear pathway between your heart and your head and never compromising what the heart wants and says. I fail at that, we all do. When you're in that space, everything else just falls into place. It's pretty simple for me.

Which individuals inspire you on the artistic level?

• Just everyone in their own way you know.

"I don't see a problem with contests at all, I just see a problem with the unbalanced amount of energy that is focused on contests and that whole way of surfing."

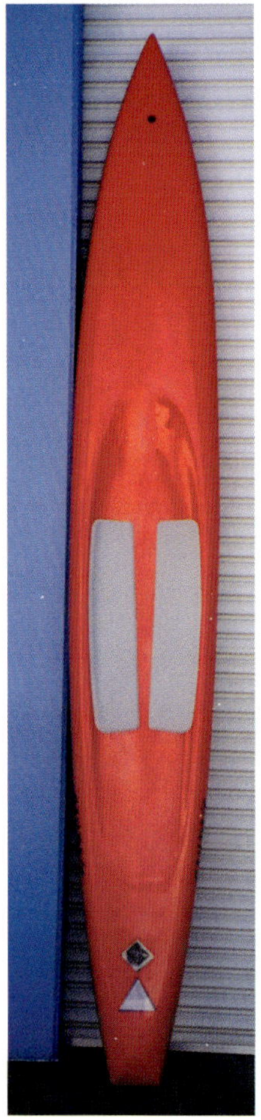

"Surfing is like golf, you ride all these different waves and you need a different board/club for each situation... If you have the pro board you can only ride it in one type of wave, ...hence the quiver."

Innovations

THE PING PONG PRINCIPLE

Dick Van Straalen, the flying dutchman of Burleigh has recently been giving the surfboard, which has reached a level of stagnation, considerable thought and has decided the only logical direction to follow is in the realm of new methods of construction. In pursuit of the harnessing of the perpetual motion of the sea more efficiently by way of faster, freer turns, Dick envisaged a board with the distinctive property of bogging down less during turns. By having less rail dragging below the surface, the surfboard would be storing more of its built up momentum for more useful explorations of the wave.

Toward that goal, several prototypes have been built utilizing forty-eight ping pong balls slotted into twelve cylindrical chambers branching out from the centerline of the halved blank.

Designers of surfboards are involved in a sport unlike any other motion sport. Riding within the coiling vortex of a hissing barrel of water is probably closer to the cosmic reality than we realize. Naturally there are going to be some characters spinning out on a tangent away from the mainstream of accepted trends. Whether a genuine practical innovation or merely a fantasy with the hope of an ever-greater loosening of our earthly ties, were it not for such experimenters we would still be walking the nose of our nine footers.

Van Straalen's innovation marginally reduces the weight of the board, but more importantly, the ping pong balls give greater buoyancy. Since ping pong balls are filled with compressed air, they provide a greater upthrust than just foam. The board's shape remains the same but the higher buoyancy created by the ping pong balls has proved it's worth, as Rabbit Bartholomew, one of Dick's test riders, confirms. "It's unreal for doing re-entries, releasing high into the air while on turns it flies out of the water. It paddles better too." Dick says the board is designed for clean days and will not go well in strong offshores or choppy conditions.

"They (the boards) have been taught to blow up due to uncontrolled ping pong fusion if you attach a leg rope," says Dick, laughing. "Seriously, they really work, and a totally better feeling will be added to your surfing."—*Martin Tullemans*

photo: Tullemans

Rabbit bouncing around on his ping pong board.

Dick Van Straalen and new innovation. photo: Merkel

' the only constant is change.' [DVS]

While Van Straalen is well recognised for being able to shape a wide variety of interesting surfcraft, he is also one who has always delved into alternative construction methods and some of them have been pretty far out...looking at the above newspaper clipping from the mid 70's titled "innovations," this is one construction method that did get some media attention, but there were plenty that didn't hit the media radar. Today epoxy resin and Styrofoam blanks are Dick's workhorse materials. Over the years he has delved into several extremely interesting alternatives; Aluminium, Carbon, and incredibly P.E.T plastics (recycled coke bottles) have all been experimented with, and the results have been outstanding. Whilst these have merely been trials thus far, all could lead down interesting new avenues in terms of design and performance. Dick is a mine of information about weight, tensile strength, motion and the attributes that these materials offer. Holding his eight foot plus carbon gun, which weighs little more than a modern shortboard, you begin to understand what he means.

'The only way we can change surfing from what it is today, is to change the materials. We are dictated to by the materials we use. The resins we are using now in this country in the surfboard industries are nearly outlawed in the rest of the world...Epoxy is the most friendly resin out there. Urethane is gas. Urethane foam are these little gas bubbles stuck together, as soon as you cut into the urethane you are releasing cyanide gas. When you look at what's coming off your urethane blank under a microscope it's like a little piece of barbed wire, it is really coarse. That's what you are taking in, whereas this (Styrofoam) is basically a shapeable plastic, it's just plastic pellets stuck together. There is no chemical in there; it's just the plastic and air. It's healthier for us, as far as the industry goes. We don't have to use the solvents. It's low emission resin, so when you are hand laminating them the resin isn't flowing into your face. Polyester is quick emission so they are going off while you are working on them. Epoxy takes about eight hours to go off, and then you are done with it and you're away from it. The foam is toxic, everything is toxic, but it's not that toxic. In the fish, the only materials we make them out of is Styrofoam and epoxy, and balsa. I haven't made any out of urethane whatsoever. It seems... what the material is, it seems to work really well with the design.'

While the Styrofoam fish is really popular Dick has also used this construction method to make epoxy/Styrofoam paddleboards for Burleigh lifeguard Mick DiBetta who won the Molaki to Oahu paddle race last year. These paddle boards have also won numerous Australian Titles and two World Titles. Even though Dick is having great success with Styrofoam and the fact that it is far healthier for the shapers to use, it seems the majority of the surfboard manufacturing industry have been hesitant in the use of alternative materials.

'It needs a different mindset, how to approach it and manufacture it. That's what people have trouble with in this industry, is accepting it. Everyone has got this mindset where they can glass a board in one day. With epoxy and Styrofoam you can't do that. You can only glass one side, and then you leave it for a day, and go back to it again. So the whole process of manufacturing, you have to change how you look at it.'

For Dick though, life goes steadily on. His little factory is not going to change, no matter what madness whirls around it. Whatever happens; even if the mainstream manage to convince the general public that surfing how and what you want for fun is just a passing fad, Dick will continue in his inexorable path of invention shaping boards for the 'average Joe,' shaping boards for his older mates to cruise on, shaping paddle boards to win world titles and shaping interesting boards for the high performance surfers too. Right now in the surf industry experimental boards are experiencing a renaissance. Dick Van Straalen has always and will always be a creative and experimental designer, and while it is in vogue for now, let us not forget the roots of this expressionism, people like Dirk Van Straalen.

crafted by Dick Van Straalen

"You take the cards that you are dealt on the day. Every day you wake up and someone deals you cards, and you go, alright there are the cards I've got for today. Next day, it's another set of cards."

one. Nat Young - Tea Tree. two. Nat Young - Honolua. three. Nat and girls. four. Rodney Sumpter - Wategos. five. Bob McTavish - Main Beach.

John Witzig was very central to Australian surfing history and particularly, documenting it, around the period of the shortboard revolution. Good mates with Nat Young and Bob McTavish and many of the stars of surfing from that era. This page contains many classic moments from the 1960's.

six. Bob McTavish and 48 Holden. seven. Matakana NZ. eight. Midget Farrelly - Main Beach. nine. Headless McTavish.

Notes From The Inner City

What you are now reading is the fifth attempt at writing this very piece, although, this version is actually very different to the four other abandoned pieces before it. Each time I have ventured into a smokey introductory first paragraph I have found that time and time again it leads me to a dead end street where all the other first paragraphs lie like rubbish on the ground.

So discarding the notion of a contrived story, I have decided to turn my mind 180 degrees and walk from that dead end street of nowhere words, where four of some fifty thousand thoughts for today are going to slowly waste away. I am stepping out to a main street of thoughts, where, flying past me go aimless words and visual teases; some driven by ego, some carried by memory, some directed by the mind, quite a few dragged along by unquestioned conditioning, and a minority motivated by pure and holy intentions.

I am letting these words just come out. An honest belch of words unhindered by a manipulative mind, coming out from another perspective that has me on the footpath in the city of my mind instead of usually standing in the main street of my thoughts being spun in a new direction, each time a speeding thought catches my minds eye.

Is everyone's mind like this? Are you always to be found in the middle of an intellectual main street? Do you and I really know the city within our skull? Where do we reside in this mental metropolis? I am on the footpath in mine, watching the steady flow of brain traffic pass me by. I am waiting, watching and wanting a ride out of town. I want to go to that place that my mind doesn't know about. That indescribable zone that you can only feel and know, but never truly understand. Outside the perimeters of the city where you only really know it by being there, and when you are not there it's impossible to describe.

As surfers we all know this place where thoughts cease and time ends. We go there via the tube; the peak experience of being in a barrel is what takes us to that blissful zone. Some people's chosen transport to the "void" is sex and for others it is music, martial arts, rock climbing and so on and so on. Yet there are also people that require no vehicle at all, no external action to take them to the blissful realm that lies beyond the confused mind. These beings are categorized by us city dwellers as, gurus, monks, yogis, and enlightened beings. Their awareness is generally situated outside the confines of the mind. They only venture into the streets of the intellectual city for practical reasons, when the amenities of the mind are truly needed. These people consciously exist and perpetually exist in a state that we only experience when we are in the tube. Imagine your life being as enjoyable as one long tube ride.

For us to have but a few seconds of this experience is enough to then devote our whole lives to chasing that "feeling". How many people on the planet do you know that remember a period of two to ten seconds, the way us surfers remember a tube ride we caught years and years ago? Personally, I know of no other activity that jams such an intense experience into such a short amount of time. Harmful drugs have the intensity, but are damaging to your body, mind and energy field. And instead of leaving you charged and full of energy and vitality, the drug leaves behind a residue of negative thoughts, painful physical effects and a shattered auric field. It is these drugs that most of us surfers out there are using to fill the hole in our lives that exists when we are not surfing. After experiencing the joyous and peaceful timeless nature of the wave and tube, we return to shore craving the opportunity to go back to that state of no mind. We search for it endlessly, be it snow boarding, rock climbing, music, drugs, drinking, the opposite sex, kite boarding, wind surfing, mountain bike riding, food, skate boarding, anything physical that might take us out of our mental city and into the spacious realm of no mind.

We look for this feeling everywhere, except where it came from.... inside of us. There are many people who believe that we are completely responsible for how we feel and react to our circumstances, and that regardless of what is happening externally we always decide for ourselves whether to feel anger, sadness, longing or joy, etc etc This is proven by looking at life around us, and how certain things that may make one person feel happiness, may make another person feel frustration. Even when the external event is exactly the same, like a surfer that puts five toes over the nose of their longboard

thoughts | Dave Rastovich
illustration | Mike Cutts

and was pissed off that they didn't get the other five over to make it ten. But for another surfer who doesn't nose ride all the time they could do the exact same hang five and be absolutely stoked, showing that the reaction to the identical experience is totally created internally. That somewhere inside us we make an almost automatic decision to react either positively or negatively, depending on our conditioning.

Owning our feelings is an important element of most eastern religions, and an invaluable tool for those of us in the west who are intuitively finding our way out of the smoggy mental metropolis. To know that you are the creator of all your feelings and out of control mental state is an incredibly empowering position to be in. No longer does the external world control your feelings and thoughts, tricking you into thinking that you have no option but to feel anger, sadness or frustration. This understanding creates all kinds of questions and possibilities about everything in life. For me the first thing I think of is tube riding. If this theory is true and that no external event creates your feelings, and that it only inspires you to feel a certain way. Then in theory I should be able to sit down and physically do nothing, yet mentally recall the experience of being barreled and self create the feeling of ecstasy, joy and no mind that I feel when riding a tube.

Choosing to now feel curious I am taking a walk around in my intellectual city. Stepping into the 'Memory Banks' to browse for any info in the way of mind mastery, I remember that when eastern mystics speak of the their experiences in meditation they actually sound like surfers who are struggling to find words to describe tube riding. Orgasmic, beyond description, only a surfer knows the feeling, no thoughts, no mind, timeless, are all words being used to attempt description of both meditation for the Yogis and tube riding for the surfers.

But how will feeling like this assist us in getting out of the endless traffic of 50 thousand daily pointless thoughts that drive around in our heads? Easy.... it's a no mind experience. We have no thoughts, no pointless internal 'chit chat' that clogs up the pathways in our brain. Meaning that the less time we spend in the mental metropolis the less noise and traffic there is. Making it easy for us to get around when we really need to use the logistical amenities of memory, language, mathematics, and science. Also at the same time, we, like the monks, yogis and enlightened beings become increasingly more receptive to what internal noise we do listen to.

Nothing is ever the same once you realise that you cannot blame anyone for how you are feeling. There is no map, no predictable path for us to take. Just intuition and complete awareness of where we are at all times, and this is what gives us excitement and enthusiasm. That sparkle in the eye of all those people you meet who are enjoying their time, is the same sparkle that you have in your eye.

Wood is Good

I would walk along the river bank watching the sunset after work and often see huge stingrays in the water just gliding along effortlessly, they had no concept of time, and I envied that. I would witness the pelicans, such a massive bird, glide from the tops of the street lamps, oh so graceful, I would find myself drifting off, imagining a wave at the river mouth, peeling forever and ever. My only hang up would be which board to ride in an effort to achieve that fantastic feeling of glide, that of the ray or the pelican. Tom Wegener has found that feeling in these timber boards, I have long admired Tom, for his style and approach to every wave, it is a tribute to his own individuality and class as a surfer. It is this that makes Tom my favourite surfer, he has influenced my surfing more than any other human, in fact I am left with only the Sting-ray and the Pelican next to this man as a direct influence on my own style.

Daryn McBride

photos: nigelARNiSON & ryanHEYWOOD

'forever is a moment and a moment is forever.'
(tom WEGENER)

The joy of wood, or indeed any kind of surfboard experiment, isn't purely in the aesthetics of the finished product; of considerably more relevance is the feel of the board where it belongs, out in the water. Positive results are currently flowing from a variety of angles. Just in our little corner of Australia: Chris Garrett's balsa fishes and thrusters, Joe Larkin's beautiful traditional mals, Van Straalen's innovation and Earthly joy's/ Balul bamboo weaves are putting people out there on partially sustainable materials, experimenting with the joy that a different feel can provide. Luke Wright is Tom Wegener's right and left hand man. Imagine immersing yourself deeply into a surfing subculture and then devoting most of your time and energy towards sustainable surfboard construction and you can feel where Luke is coming from in the following spin: *For a while there humanity relied pretty heavily on wood. Given the span of our evolution, metals and plastics only register recently on the 'materials in use' continuum. Maybe it's simply for this reason that I can't get romantic about plastic. I'm not going to get into the natural/synthetic debate; I think it's superfluous; I'm just going on observation and what I feel. Evolution has us grabbing voraciously at anything we perceive to be beneficial for our wants and needs. The advent of foam made for a broad scale clearing of anything wood in the surfboard industry, except of course for the usual role wood plays, that of a structural support, which is more often also being discarded these days. Just as single fin shortboard design lost out too soon to the twinnie, I'm sure wood was barely grasped for the possibilities in ongoing experimentation and innovation. Lightweight is right for some styles of surfing, but surely not for all?*
Given this pretence I end up where I do, making hollow construction wood surfboards with Tom Wegener. Tom takes out a full page adv in PLB 02/03, holding board No. 1 that rode for 20 minutes and sank...that's faith. What struck me was the vision: completely original (with roots in aspects of a previous time), and stemming from somewhere barely recognisable, even to himself. In a way it didn't matter where it came from, the feeling was palpable and that was enough. Now to be lost in a sea of design, learning, testing, feeling, riding stoke and primarily the versatility and beauty of wood. Seeing something new in the medium you work with everyday equates to movement, nature's pastime. What was recognisable to Tom was the way wood felt to ride. The early balsa days had stayed with him and his style of surfing required

the weight, inertia, feel, glide and speed that wood provides. Of course design principles dictate how a board will ultimately ride, and Tom as far as I can see, has love of the right design running a close second to love of his family. Being consumed by innovation means that even if a board rides well it's only a precursor to what's possible with the next one. Paradoxically, wood means your favourite board is now actually going to outlast you. Obviously not the case with balsa unless you're ultra careful, but the Paulownia we are using means the stock 12 footer, that has had dings to the wood for the last three months while we've been riding and punishing it, indicates a slight darkening of the wood directly under the ding with no absorption beyond that and no glass delamination. For mine, all I can say is that I love the feel of wood, splinters and all. Foam strikes me as inert and as a means to an end; wood conjures texture, form, kinship and every step is a beginning and an end, journey style. I'm guessing Tom sees it as such too, "**Foam is like pulling teeth, wood is just the way it is for me now.**" And swapping between the two doesn't do much for continuity, the key to progression. Since initial discussions with Paul Joske and Geoff Auer five years ago, and with two years production time passed, the fruition is perpetuating itself. The 44th board off the rank, 35th since mid '03, will be staying in house. The first personal stock since the 12' was realised at no.28, the 6' Skip inspired swallow twinnie is a gloss away from being ridden.... it's safe to say anticipation levels are getting up there. And yet off to the far left of the drive is the 5.3m lengths of milled goodness waiting to be analysed for use in the 16' Olo project, **turns out there's a few other crew who want to ride as kings.** It's true that the dream is a very niche market at the moment, however, it seems that those that know the feel like it a lot, and many converts have only needed one ride. Tom loves seeing the stoked eyes of the timber convert. As with most experimental surfing endeavours the leap of faith is the crunch point and while raising two ankle high gremmies in a new country, Tom and Margie (the local) took that leap... So, on a couple of acres a stone's throw out of Cooroy in the Noosa Hinterland, there lies an old fibro low set house, a two story wood/tin/fibro ex furniture making shed, and down in the corner is the ex chookery/piggery come mosquito breeding ground. Let's just say it's the stuff dreams are built on, not quite made of.... yet. If I had a choice of a period in surfing in which I could work it would probably be in the 70's country soul era and I've pretty much landed smack bang in the middle of it. Tom doesn't surf without a smile on his face and is working by first light, the kids run around nude under the rain water with sun glistening off crystal blonde hair, Margie's happier tending to the veggie garden than running the business in front of a computer, the acreage is planted out with 200 trees and the Kombi sounds loud. Lives aren't lives without ups and downs of course, but if the foundation is true the faith is only a feeling away. Fitting in as part of the gig stokes me inexpressibly. Creating the blanks for Tom, especially with new board ideas on the go, means plenty of design discussion over the occasional beer at the end of the day. Now that we've got the methods down we can fashion boards specifically within the confines of a jig system which primarily only restricts length. 5'6"-6'6", 9'4"-10'4" and 11'6"-12'4", are roughly the parameters at the moment but I can't see a 7' rounded pin jig being too much farther off. On the jig's we have, we've experimented with deck thickness, rail thickness, internal framing, internal sealants, rocker, foil, hip placement, board thickness etc... usually in relation to the custom order at the time. Ultimately the priority is to make an environmentally friendly long lasting board, but unless you want to oil up your stick and hang it from the rafters in a cloth bag after every surf, resin is still the go...although natural sugar and seed resins are being explored. What we have managed is pretty close to maximum internal cavity for buoyancy, this has offset the weight of the wood and means the board sits nicely in the water creating that seemingly distinctive earthly glide. It's like having an easy in with fifth gear to go to after the bottom turn. I could go on cause I love the way the boards ride and all Tommy's theories on design make logical sense to me, but I'm super green at all of this and surfers will only ever convince themselves to try something different. **I think it's safe to say that with a maturation of surfing more options will be discovered or rediscovered when it comes to design and materials.** Hopefully that maturity will include less cynicism and derision of anything left of mainstream, cause movement is good, natural is good and wood is good.

Wood is Good

'if you change, everything changes' (lucas WRIGH

Tommy Wegener's inspiration in the wood gig reflects the culmination (as well as the fresh beginning) of a lifetime's wave riding. Tommy answered the following questions on the eve of his departure for Hawaii, where he was researching into historic surf craft.

What led you to the seedlings of developing the Paulownia board?

• Paul Joske introduced me to Paulownia six years ago. I used it for stringers and fins and I found that I loved the wood. For years I thought that if I could make a pure Paulownia surfboard I would really have something special.

Has the road been long and fraught with hardship?

• Lots of hardships. The first board took about 80 hours of very hard work and it was in the water 20 minutes before being retired and basically hidden. The second board had several surfs before being cut to pieces. We had no money and couldn't afford it. The third board will be ridden for many years to come and was featured in lots of magazines and the movie "Lines from a Poem."

So what is the uniqueness of surfing a wooden board?

• Wood feels really good in the water. It is more buoyant and stiffer. You can go noticeably faster on the wave. They are heavy on land, but in the water they are light and lively. Foam is light on land but sluggish in the water.

What advantages does Paulownia offer over other forms of wood?

• First, it does not suck up salt water. Heavy wood boards are constantly getting small dings. For other wood boards, a ding is a big problem. With balsa, the wood sucks up the water like a sponge and it is very difficult to get the water out of the board. With Paulownia I have had big open dings for 6 months and there has been no water damage to the board. It is amazing. Second, there is a lot of Paulownia in Australia. Most other quality woods are becoming scarce, but Paulownia is a plantation wood that grows very fast and there are lots of plantations in Australia. Third, it is easy to shape because it has a great grain. I do most of my shaping with the block plane.

Can you ever return to foam having made this transition?

• I will never return to foam.

Recent mindset shifts in longboarding have seen people taking a renewed interest in heavy and traditional equipment; purely for the different feel it gives. In your opinion, what are the positives of the weight of your boards?

• Heavier boards are about glide. The part of glide that people who haven't riden wood don't understand is how it opens up the rideable part of the wave. The boards move much faster through the whitewash and you can make sections that would end the ride on a foam board. Also, the wood will ride higher in the wave and tube ride really well. It takes some courage to pull into a tube on a big wood board, but you have twice the horsepower to make it back out again.

Anyone trying anything new will always be vulnerable to criticism. Do you encounter a lot of closed mindedness?

• Yes, but I am pretty used to it by now. I am lucky I live in Noosa where the local crowd is small and I don't have to put up with much crap.

How has the feedback been on the wooden Skip Frye fish?

• Only one fish has been ridden and most of the riders really liked it. But, you have to be used to the retro- single fin thing to get the board right off. I find the fish to be much faster than my foam fish and the buoyancy is fun. For example when you duck dive, the board zooms you up to the surface much faster.

One of your recent projects has been the creation of two 16-foot traditional Hawaiian Olo's. Where did the inspiration for this come from?

• My wife and I have been reading the Tom Blake book. There are lots of old shots of Waikiki. It was several weeks before it dawned on me that I could easily make one of those old boards and we can surf just like them. It took five months to source the wood and make the boards. I have ridden the 16 footer a few times now and it is so fun. It is just another side of surfing that is really fun. There is bodysurfing, body boarding, short boarding, longboarding, 12 footers, and the 16 footers. If I had only one board for the rest of my life, it would be the 12 footer. But the second would definitely be the 16 footer.

'The leash slows the board down dramatically and putting one on takes some of the magic out of surfing.' tw

Is there such a thing as a template for these 16 footers? Where did you turn to for research?

• For my 16 footer, I copied the template from a photo of the Dukes hollow 16 footer that he rode in the 1930's. It has a narrow nose and a square tail. I had to pull my 12 templates out to get a nice continuous curve through the nose and middle. The tail template came from a parabolic curve from just bending wood. This is a boat curve. The front is surfboard curve while the back is a boat curve.

But, the template of the board is not really all that important. The rocker is the most important part of the shape and I really had to take a guess as to what would be right. The more rocker in the tail the easier the turn and more control, but the slower across the wave. I opted for control because a fall and lost board could be dangerous.

How have the finished articles been received, both personally and publicly?

• Not many people have seen the Olo's because they are designed to ride waves that others are not interested in. However, by the time the boards hit the water at the Noosa Rivermouth for the first go, about 20 people had gathered. We had so much fun.

Describe to me one wave on the Olo?

• My wife, Margie, and I were tandem surfing. When paddling, she lies down on the front half and her knees are on the board. About two feet behind her knees is where my head is and the rest of me is lying on the back half of the board. The regular tandem board is 4 feet shorter and ½ as buoyant as this board. We easily pick up a swell and drive across a long pealing wave together just like the couples in the old Hawaiian photos. Sharing the wave made the ride so very special. Again, this is a side of surfing that very few people have enjoyed for the last 200 years.

I've heard of you riding the 12-footer in solid waves down on the central coast. Can you see yourself riding 'bluebirds' like the duke, or is the Olo strictly a small wave escapade?

• I was so stoked on the Olo. I don't know where it will take me. I think it can handle size but the wave will have to be right. It will have to be smooth, not suck up too much, and then back off into deep water. On the biggest days at Noosa, I have sat way wide of the point and taken the bommies on the 12 footer and now it will be much better on the Olo. You know, the thing about traditional longboarding stoke is that it is very easily achievable. You can read the Hawaiian legends of surfing, then the Duke's stories, and paddle right out to the breaks they rode. It is easy. You can go to the museums and some of the restaurants and touch their original surfboards. You can go to the beach and talk to the living legends. It is complete Stoke.

As far as the scale of your project goes, can you see yourself expanding, or will it remain as a home and family based operation?

• Wegener Surfboards will not expand. So many other shapers have gone the production way and they tend to regret it. Luke (who works for me) and I are it and we have a goal of 50 wood boards a year. That is it.

Have you had much interest from overseas?

• Almost nobody has heard of the 12 footers overseas yet. There are no stories or photographs until the recent Surfers Journal story by Phil Jarrett. We just shot with Thomas Campbell for the last two weeks for his new movie, "Sprout". I only rode the 12 footer. His movie should be another blockbuster for the traditional surfing scene and it will hopefully help get the word out on the 12 footer. Thomas calls the stoke from the big boards the "fever". He ordered a wood board while he was here.

The final threshold of creating a board from sustainable materials seems to be the resin and glass. Have you come across any viable alternatives to the standard?

• No, but I would love to find an environmentally perfect alternative. However, good old resin and fibreglass is pretty ideal for the wood boards. It is easy to repair, shines up nicely, gives a nice hard shell to the wood, and lasts a long time. The wood will last longer, and in 20 years or so you can sand back the resin and redo the glass job. When I am done with making a wood board, the offcuts of wood heat my house in winter, the sawdust goes on the garden and there is a minimal waste of resin and glass. The waste that goes in the bin is about the same as the waste from a McDonalds lunch.

Do you perceive surfing in general as going down a more experimental route, with more people aiming to have fun, as opposed to 'rip'?

• I don't know. Since I have been surfing, there always has been the mainstream and the offshoots in surfing. The main stream dominated the press, but there were always the undercurrents. Now the undercurrents are getting more press. The biggest change that I have seen is girls are getting into surfing. I think they add a nice balance and friendly vibe to the water."

Beer: Australian, American or European????

• I love beer. I usually drink light or mid-strength so I can enjoy more volume. I buy whatever is on special.

Tommy recently featured in Thomas Campbell's new movie 'Sprout.' Gliding on timber is getting positive feedback from a wide audience. As a surfer, Tom is inspirational and free. While Dan Wozniak's film 'Siestas and Olas' isn't as successful as it should be, perhaps the pendulum is swinging to this other side of surfing style...and hopefully long lasting surfcraft.

Tom Wegener is available for custom orders and correspondence:
wegener@switch-foot.com

Wood is Good

On Safari
Nigel Arnison

nigelarnison

Somewhere between night and day there's a time when light appears less defined, like you're enveloped rather than pointed at. At dawn and dusk there exist moments of seemingly shadowless light when your senses are gently relieved of their preoccupation with focus. I was only ever aware of the more obvious shades in the light spectrum until I met Nigel Arnison. 'Nige' is a photographer with a penchant for light and form in the natural environment, particularly the ocean, specifically waves.

Now Nige would be the first to admit he hasn't been up before 9am for months, however here on the Sunshine Coast we've had a wave spell that's pretty much driven every surfer nuts, let alone photographers who shoot waves for a living. So at the moment Nige works hard on alternative travel images and enjoys his other passion for music, while his partner Sally sells the best back catalogue and documentation of waves on the Sunshine Coast ever assembled via markets and the website.

After studying photography in Brisbane, Nige moved north on a whim, the work on the trawlers was getting a bit much and shifting circumstances seemed like an illogical thing and a kick up the creative backside. Shooting the natural environment was the primary focus and the opportunities at the local Eumundi markets for photographers back then were certainly better than today. Although Nige occasionally had the ocean as a feature in the past it was the recalling of early Stradbroke trips and the persistent suggestion from local surfer Jacob Stuth to focus on the wave that prompted the niche work. Then it became about the moment.

With waves there are rarely second chances, he knows it's there but it'll take a two hour session in the water at the same time everyday to get the shot, and as if the conditions will be the same the next day, Huey hardly works like that even in the most stable of climates. So it's the thrill of the chase and rewards are brilliant; when they come. Coordinating the ingredients for a shoot is a long checklist that falters as soon as one slice of the pie is missing. Given a (decent size) swell window in any given year from 4-10 weeks, when it's on; everything else is off.

The prints he's sold in the last two months will fund the film and processing for the next two days, but what a rush when it comes together. Capturing the essence of the energy involved as the most beautiful the ocean has to offer, while highlighting the hundreds of characters found in wave form and those that ride them.

Any true artist will tell you that the creative process is a reciprocal relationship. The validation for Nige is in the look on the surfer's face when he sees his local break firing the way he remembers it, or initially when a roll comes back and 'that image' in his head is superseded by the one on the light box, and then there's the stoke in the water as the timing of surfer, wave, light and camera meld to capture a unique documentation of a time and place in surfings varied history. So he gets his and we get ours, just take a look.

By Luke Wright

Oh Safari

Surfing Photographic
Nigel Arnison

jacobstuth

Jacob Stuth is one surfer that Nigel has been on many surfing surfaris with. Using his beloved beach buggy, a frequent event for Jake would involve getting back to the Dreamtime years of catching dinner and surfing alone, in a zone that is timeless and still readily available today. The surfing safari is an experience for all surfers and literally what many surfers live for...that next chase. Travelling to remote locations, scoring perfect waves (with no-one out) and getting back to the roots of the search. It is more than just riding the waves though... It is the whole trip...when on safari with Jacob it is a trip. Making time to be 'away' and meeting Jake (fully loaded) in his beach buggy...the trip begins...hustling up some camping equipment...grabbing some food stuff...maybe a fishing rod...leaving the modern day attachments and driving away...not knowing where...but knowing why. It is an escape, much like the surfing experience, to put you in a zone that alienates daily pressure/stress to the obsolete pile. It's the acoustic guitar over campfire nights, listening to the serenity of waves crashing to their resting place, while you are resting on the sand, anticipating the morning glass. It's the sunrise with foreign birds chirping and waking to an environment that is an eon away from inner city blues. Aside from all the joys of embracing primate behaviour and turning loose, being free from the fear of society's expectations, the surfing safari hopefully leads to riding waves. After experiencing a few idyllic surfing safaris, it is easy to understand how some surfers can walk away from society in general and lead a hermit lifestyle close to their love and local wave. Some say that Jacob has chosen this path and I don't think many could blame him, but for envy.

Jacob: "Riding old boards over the years has been similar to studying a hydrodynamics degree at university. Riding boards with different foils, rockers, fin position, fin shape and foil, outlines, thickness, length. Riding old single-fins in challenging powerful waves is a great way to learn fast about style, weight placement and positioning yourself in the pocket, the place that all good Surfers' spend most of their time. Russel Graham from Torquay has a wonderful collection of surfboards from all eras. Over the years Russ has offered me many old classics to ride with the understanding that I would give him a full evaluation of the shape and how it rode Bells that day. Waves I have ridden over the years have dictated my style today and the way I ride waves relates to experience gathered from skating, snowboarding, skiing and dancing. Surfing for me is expressionism, dancing, artistic, socialising and meditation."

"Surfing is many things to many people. Over the years surfing has been a sport, an exercise, a workout, a cleanser, a healer, meditation, a place to think about life, a place to meet friends and make new ones. Being a surfer is a state of mind. To surf is one way to cope with society's expectations and pressures. The ocean is the greatest lover since Jesus. The ocean heals all who enter her. She offers joyful moments amidst chaotic whitewash."

' a man travels the world over in search of what he needs, and returns home to find it.' [georgeMOORE]

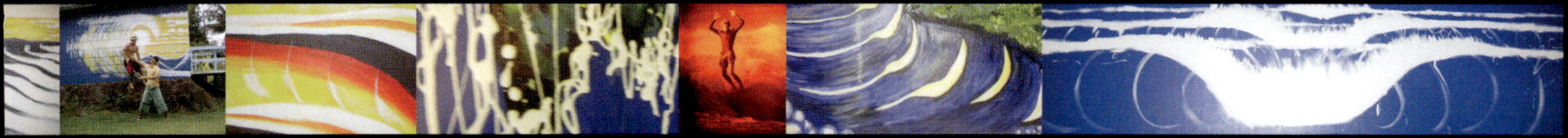

Oh Safari
Nigel Arnison

Mal Sutherland Photo

Born and bred in Queensland, Mal Sutherland was surfing in the 1950's, established the Kirra Boardriders club in the 1960's and is still involved with surfing today. Though Mal was usually surfing on the good days, you can see there are some timeless images here.

five. Cooper @ Byron. six. Noosa 1964. seven. Snapper Rocks. eight. Rainbow Bay.

jimBANKS

Jim Banks hardly needs any introduction. A fearless and talented surfer, Indo and beyond pioneer, one-time bronzed Aussie, health guru, musician, shaper, and philosopher; he is the definition of someone who has lived his life by the oceans beat. Furthermore, he is one of those rare people who constantly considers, contemplates and reflects on all aspects of his time spent on the earthly plane. In this contribution Jim briefly reveals a portion of his perception of the surfing experience.

Surfing is one of the most intimate experiences a person can have with nature. To be picked up on a wave of energy that has travelled for (sometimes thousands of) miles across the ocean and carried effortlessly towards the shore is an exceptionally unique experience. Every time I've witnessed somebody taste this for the first time, they've burst into a state of pure joy. Laughing, screaming, yahooing and, as fast as possible, heading straight back out for more. For those who are lucky or experienced enough to ride deep inside the spiralling vortex of a tube that flies across a bed of golden sand or multicoloured coral reef, it's an experience that is usually life changing. Many surfers give up their sports, their girlfriends, their hometowns and their careers to seek out opportunities and relationships that are better suited to pursuing this profoundly powerful experience with nature.

The world at large has always had some sense of this, a feeling that what surfers are doing is very special, very powerful and totally unique. The surfers, the magazines and the movies of the 50's, 60's and early 70's, full of adventure, rebelliousness and reckless abandon captured and portrayed this. Often to the point where straight society, clinging to their flimsy and rigid values like shipwrecked mice in the ocean of existence, felt threatened by surfers' flagrant disregard for many of their values. The surfers' deeper connection with nature had also, inadvertently, brought them to a deeper connection with the truth itself.

When professional surfing reared it's beady eyed head in the late 70's the writing was on the wall, although not too many saw it. Competitive surfing's grab for dollars came with a price. And the price was surfing's soul. Surfing was led astray from it's adventurous quest for the truth; it's celebration of individual uniqueness and purity of expression. Hand held down the narrow corporate road of conformity, surfing was homogenised, sterilised and packaged for the masses. It's paid off big time for a select few players. But if you look closely along the side of the road, you can see that it's littered with the bodies and broken hearts of many talented and spirited surfers. Off in the distance, the footsteps of many of surfing's most talented and visionary disciples disappear into the wilderness, their words of wisdom and gifts of genius ignored in the bloody frenzied grab for dollars.

I live in hope that surfing will recover it's lost soul and become that great adventure, celebration of uniqueness and a purity of expression that captured my heart and soul in the early seventies. A place where how we feel becomes more important than how good we are or who we defeated. And I'm not talking about the feeling of personal self-gratification here, but about the feeling of being at peace and in harmony with the people and the environment around us. About the feeling of being aligned with our spirit and our purpose in life. The feeling of not compromising ourselves, our environment, or those around us... The feeling of understanding the importance of celebrating the beauty and magnificence of creation itself.

This is what surfing is, a celebration of life and creation. It is a dance, an expression of feelings and emotions and personal style. It is a dance of great power that has the ability to transform all those who come into contact with it. It can be the dance of testing oneself, of our ability to understand and move across a moving, spinning wall of water. Sometimes it can be a dance of testing our fear and our ability to survive, treading the fine line between life and death itself as played out in the giant waves of Hawaii or the bone crushing reefs of the South Pacific and Indian oceans.

The Future

Surfing may be about to be freed. Freed from the narrow path that competitive corporate surfing has held it ransom to. The net may just save surfings' soul. It is well possible that no longer will dollar hungry corporations and their heavily compromised media slaves dominate surfings' image. Now individuals freely can express previously suppressed voices easily and effectively via the net, without being compromised by demographics, advertising dollars or limited editorial space. No longer do you need a huge advertising budget or editorial muscle to have your say. Providing the world can find you!

This will become the key in the future, being able to be found and heard amongst the millions of sites that litter the net. This is where a freeform collective can be so effective. It can become a powerful channel for uncompromised and non-commercially oriented voices to have their say and be heard. A place that people can trust to go to and receive non-commercially distorted information. A place where surfing's artists and visionaries can be seen and heard.

People are naturally drawn to powerful expressions of spirit. Large rock concerts, and the seat filling power of actors like Jack Nicholson stand testament to this. The net may be just the opportunity that surfing needs to reclaim it's birthright - as an incredibly unique and powerful expression of spirit that touches the heart and soul of everyone who comes in contact with it. Via the net, surfing now has the opportunity to be portrayed with a depth and integrity that can lift it out of the narrow paradigm that it's been trapped in and allow it to stand tall in this exponentially changing world.

Photo: ryanHEYWOOD

While George Greenough is more famous for his film-making, surfboard design and innovation, he is also a world class still photographer. These photographs are all from his collection, a collection that was only skimmed over unlike many of the other legends of the lens. If people like George's photographs hopefully it will encourage further exploration into his library. Check out the story on Dolphin Glide to get a further feel for this man's photographic eye.

one. Unknown KIWI - Noosa 1966. two. McTavish - Noosa 1965. three. Black wave. four. McTavish - Double Island Pt 1965. ards.

five. Hollister Ranch. six. Nat - Channel Islands. seven. Lennox - Circa 1969. eight. Bob riding the baby - Circa 1968 - CW. nine. San Juan - Byron 1968. ten. McTavish - Noosa 1965.

art Retrospective

Garry Birdsall was born in Sydney where surfing is a national pastime. He spent all of his leisure time as a youth on the beaches of Sydney. He was one of the pioneers of Malibu surfboard riding, and has participated in numerous Australian and world surfing events. He was the first artist worldwide to do air-brushed paintings on surfboards. Garry's re-creation of "Surfing in the 60's" is an authentic, historical depiction of surfing scenes of that era.

retro revival

Focusing on experimental board design: with words from Bob McTavish, Dick Van Straalen, Beau Young, Dain Thomas, Neal Purchase, Andrew Kidman, Dave Rastovich and George Greenough.

KIWI pioneer - darynMcBRIDE (circa pre-fashion)
Photo: jacobSTUTH

When I was talking to Bob McTavish about the future of the shaping industry, surf tech and mass-produced boards definitely came into the conversation. Asking McTavish whether he thought in another 20 years there would be anyone around who could shape a variety of boards; he said the following;

"Fortunately we have the Dain Thomas's and the Ben McTavishs' of this world. They are the two I know right away who are here who can do that work. Dain is 25, Ben is 27, and they can do a board from start to finish. They want to understand the entire thing. They can do the whole lot. Fortunately there is a young generation of shapers coming through who are not interested in being pop-out, mass production shapers."

Dain Thomas is like the opposite of mass production, he makes boards at home under his "Sea" label and he also plugs away shaping in the McTavish factory (in Byron Bay) to make ends meet. "Sea Surfboards" is Dain and his buddy Matt Yates keeping it grass roots. They have a shaping bay at their country farmhouse, they shape, they paint and they design boards with creative inspiration coming from the past, the future and abroad. The whole concept of "Sea Surfboards"is a timeless surfers dream... If you wound the clock back 30 years nothing has changed, Bob McTavish would have been doing the same thing; shaping boards at the farm with some of his buddies finishing it off with a touch of artwork and that is exactly what is happening today with 'Sea' and other small scale operations. It really brings home that the lifestyle of working, shaping and surfing is still a realistic option if you have the passion and the focus.

Due to the competitive nature of the shaping business these days, factory production of surfboards has to be just that, factory production. It is very difficult to put something new through the system; it takes more time to do a one-off shape and time is money. Without individuals in the surfing industry, experimentation with surfboard design would continue along the factory process of conformation.

"A lot of good designs have been overlooked because they are difficult to manufacture. To make a lot of surfboards of just the one design, it doesn't really make sense to do it by hand, and keep it handcrafted. It's a pretty manufacturing friendly design we are at today, the standard shortboard, and standard longboard. I also believe that there are a heap of designs scattered throughout surfboard design history that shouldn't be made obsolete.' (Dain)

The mass production of surfcraft is a reality in the 21st century. Factory produced surfboards will indisputably always have a place in the global market from now on. At one end of the spectrum of modern surfboard creation is a giant company churning out hundreds of identical boards everyday and at the other end of the spectrum is a ray of sunshine hitting a country shaping bay.

'There will always be people who want a handcrafted surfboard with their name pencilled on the stringer, something they've been able to watch being created, having me think about them while I'm shaping it has some effect on the energy of the object. All of a sudden it is not an inanimate object; it has been created with a certain person in mind, with passion. There will always be a place for handcrafted surfboards.' (Dain)

Dain began shaping Sea surfboards because he could not find the boards he wanted to ride anywhere else. Today he is very involved with shaping full time at the McTavish factory, and for a country kid, he is well up-to-speed with the cutting edge of board design in the States, (with mates like Steve Lis and Thomas Campbell) and he translates all this information into functional surf craft for his local waves in Northern NSW.

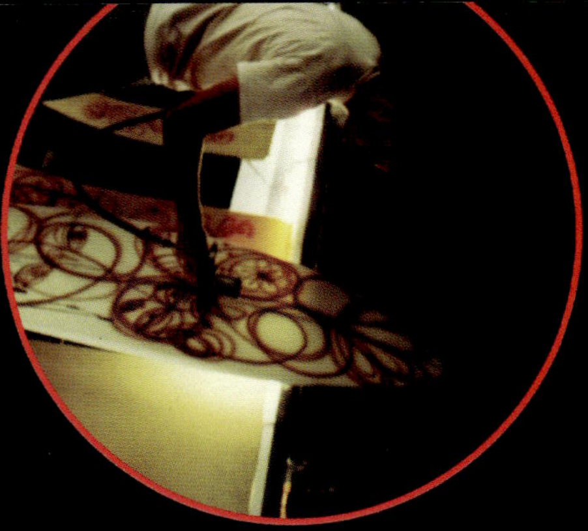

A recent visit from Steve Lis has led to a batch of new templates, and fascinating new designs. The quad fin, five-fin, bonzer, twin-keeled fish, and widow-maker are all part of Dain's shortboard repertoire. As far as long-boards go, he is a master of heavy flat logs built for section connection and noseriding ease. Asking Dain how much Steve Lis helped him he said the following;

"Steve helped immensely in the fish department. Before I hung out with Steve I was just mimicking what Skip Frye was doing and what I thought worked, but Steve really outlined how they work, why they are so fast and why they are great down the line. He isolated all the principles and explained what gave the design it's flavour and how it is possible to refine them. He helped me out heaps. It changed the way I shaped the fish immensely."

Within surfing, the 'retro revival' is alive and well; old ideas being borrowed and mixed with a new age of hybrids that in many ways are a VERY positive thing for our 'sport.' With more people experimenting and riding different surf craft it can do nothing but help sow the seeds of individualism and individualism breeds evolution, which breeds change... and change is healthy. Let's hope that change in board design helps to encourage changes in the water, with people surfing for fun and having fun. There is a whole 'other side of surfing.'

To round off (the nose of) this story on surfboard design I have found surfers and shapers that I know are developing surfboards that are not only functional but also surfboards that bring out the style aspect of surfing; an aspect that is slowly being lost to performance.

Dain: "You take the best from the old school and leave the shit behind."

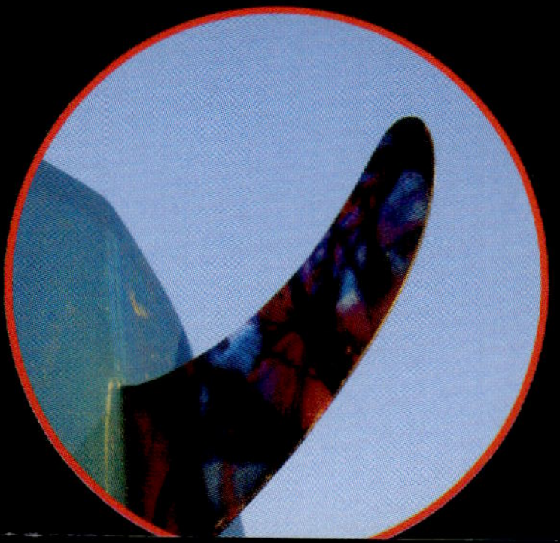

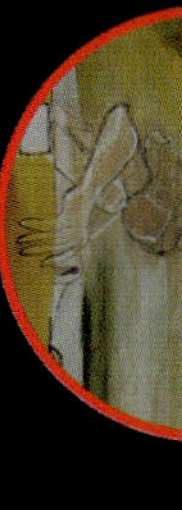

Artwork by: Matt Yates, Harry the Hat & Thomas Campbell.

BOARD DESIGN

' what we have to learn to do, we learn by doing.' [ARISTOTLE]

What motivated you to move towards further experimentation with surfboard design?

Kidman: "Dave Parmenter and I guess surfing with Derek (Hynd) at J-Bay."

Purcho: "Just seeing the style of the surfers (and my old man) in those old magazines and particularly watching some of the old movies and it was just new and inspiring…it's the style and the grace and the way the boards ride the barrel. These days it is all about the manoeuvre and I get bored of that, I like the barrel."

Rasta: "Boredom (much laughter). I saw the value at a very early age of being a little more creative and putting your neck out a little bit and trying something different, just to see how it goes."

Beau: "Always been interested in it. Andrew Kidman kind of got me into the small side fin set up, just talking about Dave Parmenter and the widow maker and that mid face holding in rather than skipping out effect and I was trying to figure it out…now I have."

Van Straalen: "I never went the thruster set up, I never liked it…didn't like the way they surf, I just kept riding single fins and tri fins…because a single fin is really drivey and I think maybe the bottom turn is becoming fashionable again, because the bottom turn, (due to thrusters) has been cut out a lot. You don't see many people really laying it over on their bottom turns."

Why are all these kids (that are learning to surf) riding the same board that the top 44 are trying to win the world tour with, when they are just going to the beach for a paddle?

Purcho: "It's because it's the only food they're being fed mate. It's all through the marketing of the corporate companies, owning the advertising spaces and demanding stories on their surfers and filling up all the magazines with the same shit. There is more to surfing than that, and that's what is not being brought out to them…the only way kids learn is by seeing and looking at stuff and they just don't get to see it. They're just not fed anything different."

Beau: "Probably for the same reasons that say Neal or I rode them when we were younger. It's because that's where all the media is directed, that's where the advertising is and that's where all the money is directed…purely at that form of surf craft. You know, everyone is taking the pill and all riding those boards…that's their decision and they are welcome to it."

Dain: "It's solely because that's the style of surfing they grew up watching, that's how they want to surf and that's who they want to emulate. Kids see it and they want to do it. That's all they see."

Rasta: "Its all about low risk, they see a large number of people all riding the same thing, so the consumer assumes that is the best thing to buy and that there is low risk in losing money or getting a shit board. The surfing media doesn't provide much option either as far as surf-craft goes…who cares anyway?"

Kidman: "We all had it when we were kids. You're a kid and that's what you want. It doesn't matter. When you're a kid (and you're growing up) you want the coolest brand. I remember my dad saying to me, 'what do you want that for, it's just an advertisement for the company.' You can't tell your kids though… and the companies know that… and you know what? Who gives a shit anyway?"

What design things are you working with at the moment since you gave up the ideals of the performance thruster setup?

Purcho: "Thrusters have their place in a certain type of wave. For me the way I want to surf is to feel glide and hold the rail for a long time and those Dave Parmenter influenced 'widows' (big middle fin with two stabilisers) for me are the perfect board when it gets good...you can come off the bottom and you can get it really low, really hang it over and still have that same single fin glide down the face...and they hold in the tube just unreal because they got that big back fin still and they just get that amazing glide through the barrel you know. The modern rails are a lot better than they had in the 70's. Aside from rails and bottom curves, basically I have just gone thicker and wider."

Kidman: "Fins, I am really into my fins. People are really into this fish thing, but I'm not sold on them here in Queensland, I don't think they work well in the sort of waves we have here. Neal's (Purcho) old man is shaping fishes that work well here, but they are so different to a Skip Frye fish in every respect. That's why Neal's dad's boards are so good too; because he went through all that shit in the 70's...he puts all the stuff he has learned into them too. What are you asking me for anyway? You should be asking Deanie (Wayne Dean)."

Beau: "I think there are a lot of people now that understand the principle of surfing smoothly. I love watching the aesthetics of Neal's surfing and Andrew and Dain and a lot of guys on twin fins...it seems to draw out their surfing...not like cramping up, they just seem to flow a lot more and let everything intertwine with the waves, rather than cutting little strips at it you know...it's like a smooth line and big arc...it's pretty and really pleasing to watch for me. It forces you to hold your rail on that line, it's rail surfing...it's not any easier or any harder, it's just different."

Dain: "As far as design goes, nothing that earth-moving, just lots of little refinements. I am refining the fishes too and going wider and lower volume, but keeping the same outline. Playing around a lot with fins too (particularly foils) and perhaps in the future we will see variable foils? Materials are a big one, finding cheaper and more environmentally friendly ways of constructing a surfboard."

Van Straalen: "The biggest thing I always say is that we can't change surfing until we change the materials and the materials dictate to us how we surf. So, when you look at new materials it opens up new possibilities because they are going to go different and you shape them different and this is what a lot of people don't take into consideration. It's the same as Styrofoam and we know how it works and that is why we shape the fish out of Styrofoam, because the fish likes the extra cork. Van Straalen: "I liken everything a lot to music, there's not a lot of music that you listen to today that will stand the test of time...the widow maker has stood the test of time, so it must be good...so is the fish that was started in the mid 60's for example."

It is good seeing Purcho and Beau Young being influenced by another style of surfing... that generation of their fathers...because their fathers surfed a totally different way. They look at their fathers surfing and it really makes them think. Without that link to the past we wouldn't be doing what we are doing today.".

All photos: mattyYATES

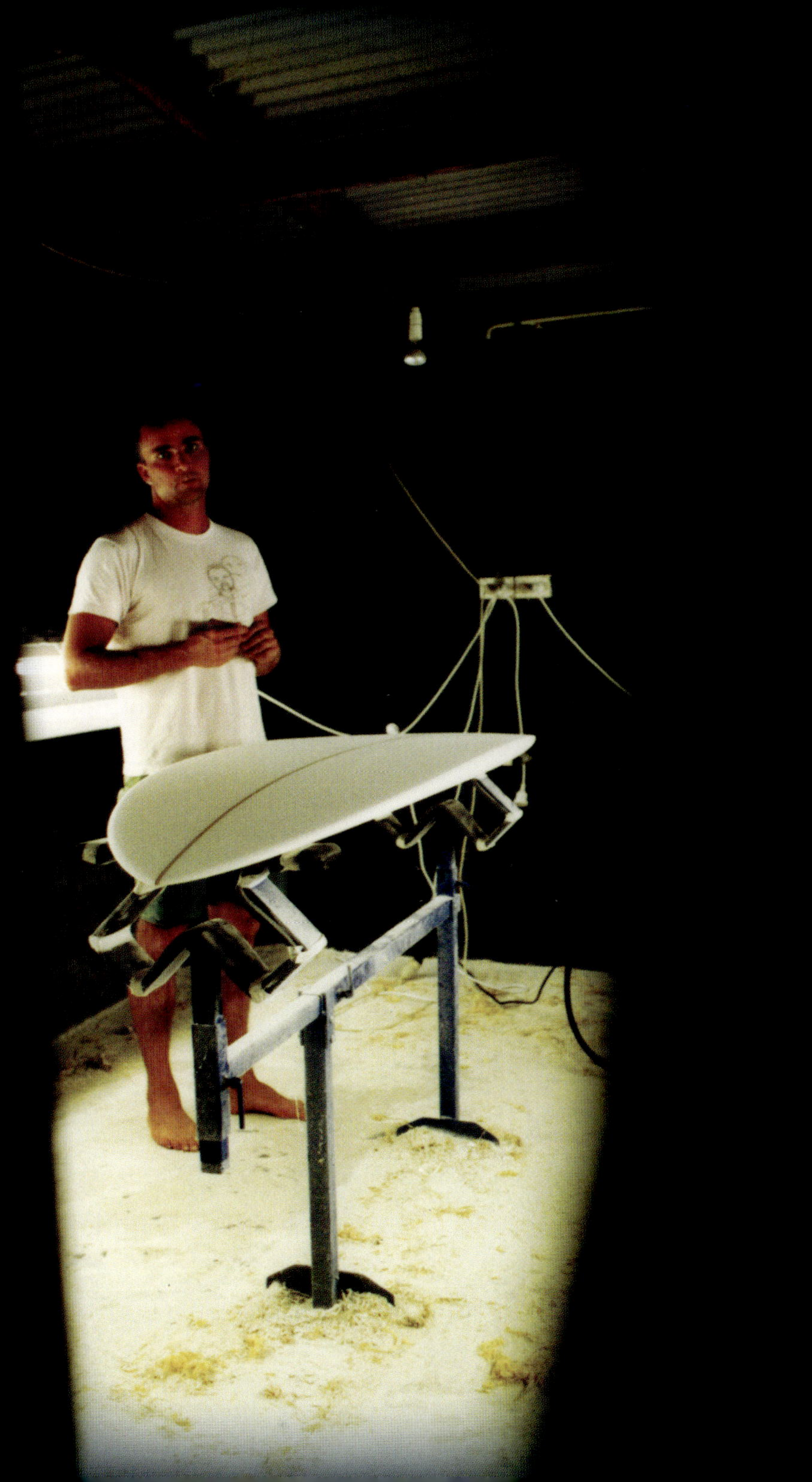

' the life so short, the craft so long to learn.' [HIPPOCRATES]

Californian monster child in Australia: TC

• if i have seen further it is by standing on the shoulders of giants •

Artwork: alexKROPP (big gay al)

Laurie McGinness was central to Surfing World magazine in the 1970's as one of the chief photographers and writers. While contributing to other surfing publications and compiling books, Laurie collaborated with his mate Peter Crawford to compile one of his finest publications, the hardcover book WILDWATER – The Surfriding way of life. Further images can be viewed on the website.

one. PT @ Backdoor. two. Rabbit @ Pipe. three. MR.

four. PT Soul arch/Style master.

SURFTRAVEL-CAPTIONS

' if you're not living good...travel wide.' [bobMARLEY] image | nigelARNISON

« Real surfers never stay home ». I've been trying to become a real surfer for 20 years now and after 60 dedicated surftrips in 30 countries, I guess I've shared a bit of diversity of this surfing world although I still miss main places like Hawaii, Japan, Mentawaii or New Zealand on my list. One of the most wonderful aspects of travelling is to meet all kinds of people. It matters to feel how much you can trust and what you can expect from people. More often than not, bumping into characters and locals is a positive experience and surfing is full of weirdos, or at least unusual individuals. On the top of surfing stories, surfers love chatting about anecdotes which made their surf trip different than any other trip and the combination of surfing conditions and transport is enough to make any surftrip worthwhile, whether it is on the other side of the world or next door. Here are a few of those anecdotes.

Antony "yep" Colas

www.lowpressure.co.uk

Surf Guides? Why?

For a long time, surfing guides have been banned by the hardcore surf community. The rule of thumb was that any travelling surfer should shut up about spot names they would discover. That was the time of the great discoveries in the 60's and 70's (Bali, G-Land, Nias, Baja, Puerto Escondido, Taghazout, Costa Rica, Fiji) by the pioneers of surftripping (Peter Troy, Craig Peterson, Kevin Naughton, Randy Rarick...). Stories run in Surfer Magazine would give only vague clues about locations. This editorial guideline remains until now and has been followed by most surfmags in the world. In the meantime, Surfer Mag started a low-key surf travel publication aimed at providing a worldwide spot data to the travelling community. Since 1981, The Surf Report has published over 200 monthly issues around the world, reaching an estimated coverage of 80% of the surf shores with a full description of spot access, wave features and travel specifications.

Whereas the surfmag's publishing policy hasn't changed much over the last 20 years, the worlwide surf community has been booming because surfing is a fabulous sport enhanced by an ever growing culture of sports and travel combined with a society focused on freedom. While the ISA's figure of 18 million surfers might seem overrated, there is no denying that potential travelling surfers have reached millions. Such figures require some kind of management. A growing portion of surf travellers are relying now on surf operators: camps & schools, tours & boats, operators and agents...The global surfing zone is extending towards boat access breaks, secluded camps in dangerous areas, high latitude cold water destinations...Waveriders need a relevant tool to manage their trip whether they go on their own or with an operator. If they only rely on well-known spots published by surfmags or contest sites, that means most surfers would gather to a very limited number of the major spots which would be overcrowded. Not telling about spots favors that ugly territorial behavior known as Localism. Some locals think they own the spot because they surf there all the time, assuming nobody will ever break their privilege. Funnily enough, the same guys who blame surfing guides telling about their own private garden, are the happy users of surftravel books when they travel abroad. We heard the very same surfers despise surfmags articles and confess they got hooked on surfing by looking at a picture in a mag. Basically, the local's theory is : 'I've started surfing or I surfed that spot before you, it's okay for me and my friends to surf there but you are a kook or too late, just leave.' It's high time to discourage that selfish behavior.

The idea of a surfmap, according to our ethics, is to increase the spot's public knowledge, let's say to 90%. But not 100%. If you take a zone of 10 potential spots, there has to be at least 1 spot off the map, formerly referred as " the secret spot ". Real secret spots in most wavezones don't exist any more as such, some waveriders know this place but it's been kept low key for several reasons : tricky access, inconsistent break, land or wave dangers...The map provides a graphic info base for the waverider to search the coastline and get curious about both underwater and land topography. The global guideline is to enhance the waverider towards knowledge of the wave, the place and the people. Safety is a big issue and waveriders have to be aware of the local dangers. Thus, flows of waveriders are better orientated depending on their skills, their wave tools and their ability to take risks. Spot types favor a better distribution of waveriders so anyone finds his Mecca. Example : worldclass, pointbreak, rivermouth, cliff reefbreak, swell magnet, big wave reef, mushy beachbreak, secret, longboard heaven, beginner's beach, bodyboard'shorebreak, jetty break, experts only, sucking hardbreaking ledge, kid's playground... What is yours ?

The World Stormrider Guide is only a pre-guide, not a practical guide. It's not designed to be used as a travel guide on-site but as a decision tool to find out about where, when and why to go on a surftrip. Then, you need to get a practical guide as well as a surfing guide. We recommend Lonely Planet for their in-depth information, cultural aspects as well as their commitment in surfing sections for some countries.

We do that job because first, we love surfing and travelling. Thus, we want to be able to stay as close to the waves as possible getting a decent income. We believe publishing information about spots is not a crime. Of course, it has it's downside on the surf environment like every human activity involved in production but it can also mean a better surfing future. It's called positive evolution. Be convinced we will use part of our energy to protect what we live for and do our best to educate surfers, who are not always careful of their trips' local impact. What will become an absolute priority in the near future, unlike other sketchy characters that could develop the same business with less eco-concerns and more interest towards money, power and glory. Surfspots are increasingly in danger and lobbies involved with harbor development, fishing industry and even tourist industry can take over some spots or deny access, it's high time for dedicated surfers to act as a group. Like the Surfrider Foundation and other environmental surfers groups have been doing with all kinds of wave-users.

Antony "yep" Colas

Sri Lanka. May 1999.

smart thief

I'd been warned against the Siam Hotel in Arugam Bay where robberies had occurred. But it was cheap and well located. Somehow, I found out that $100 had disappeared from my wallet. It was a pretty subtle thievery but $100 made a gap in my budget. I did a thorough search, stating that I was gonna report to the police. Apparently the thief had gone and spent the money. I maintained pressure and most of the cash was turned back. So I could rent a bike to check the surrounding spots and wildlife as well as taking a daytrip by boat to Crocodile Rock. Nothing around rivals A-Bay when this consistently small right pointbreak gets over 4-5ft.

Galapogas / Ecquador March 2004.

bloody consistent surf.

I damaged my back severely, snapped my only board which I purchased a week before in Guayaquil and destroyed a camera body but still, San Cristobal was a blast. It's a dream surfers' harbor town. It holds a worldclass right and great lefts on both sides of a laid back village. And backup spot Loberia is a powerful A-Frame in the middle of a live zoo. Seals are the kings. Fish are plentiful so they spend little time feeding. Most of the day, they bask in the sun, mate with a female and ride a lot of waves. More than a dolphin, I'd like to be a seal out there in my next life.

Senegal. Nov 1997.

bloody consistent surf.

The Almadies Peninsula holds 95% of the surf in the whole country. We drove north to St-Louis and South and never found evidence of consistent good surf whereas Dakar Tip acts as an amazing swell magnet with plenty of quality reefbreaks. Spot density is an issue when you can walk to more than 10 spots with an exposure range of 220°, which means you can always surf offshore conditions. But you have to deal with cunning natives on the beach, who make you feel guilty about their position. Endless hassle is the rule. But that's only if you're French.

Gabon. Feb 1996.

one-wave trip and malaria.

When I saw that aerial picture of Olendé, my heart immediately started racing. I tried to organize my first trip with pro riders and photographer. Many cancelled but a team of 4 finally got there. Wrong season, it's too obvious now but I did not realize how outseasoned we were then. We surfed a few 1-2ft punchy beachbreaks most of the time, and suddenly a 3ft left set came out of the blue and I caught one. That was the only decent wave in 10 days. The trip down to Olendé was either 12hr with risky canoe or 1hr power boat costing $4000. We cancelled the trip ! We were to carry on to Congo but Air Gabon fucked up with our tickets. Not so unfortunate when I discovered back home I had caught malaria (Falsiparum type) : 4 days in hospital.

Port Gentil.

Pakistan.

Galapogus.

Cape Nada.

Tarrapac, Chile.

Tavarua.

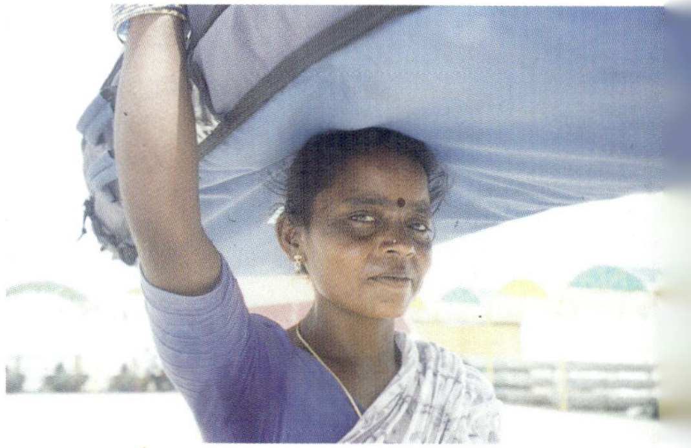
India.

Dera Lefts.

Pakistan.

Ponta Ruiva, Portugal.

SURFTRAVEL-CAPTIONS

Avalanche, France.

Cloud 9.

Gustharx, France.

Madeira. Feb 1998.

classic session missed.

We drove around a lot, being ready for those big rights on the south coast or those nice lefts on the north coast. Always breaking on the rocks. Swell showed up at some stage but nothing outstanding. My good friend Nicolas was to fly back home on a Sunday. We left that day and Jardim was flat. The tied board bags went off the roof and almost killed someone. A stop at Machico revealed decent windswell action but it was time for Nicolas to check in and we checked the NE coast afterwards with an obvious rising swell. We were told then that Jardim had 2 hours of perfect surf in the evening. Next morning, we woke up at dawn, watched 2 sets then the ocean went flat for days.

Great Ocean Road. April 2001.

ring the bells

Thanks to Surf Session/Rip Curl, I got a free flight to attend the Bell's Beach contest. I got there for the Quarters and the surf was pumping. I was shooting sideways from Winkipop alongside another cameraman. He noticed a "Stormrider's Club " sticker on my camera and says : "hey, it's funny, I made a movie called Stormriders 30 years ago." The guy was Dick Hoole. I love those random meetings, I tried to explain to him what Stormriding means. Then, Tony Ray's father showed up : great chats and great show. Wildcard Fanning wins in front of a very experienced crowd of people who really know surf contest heats. Despite the proximity of Melbourne, the Great Ocean Road is such a well-protected area.

Côte Basque. Since 1983.

home polluted home.

My homebreak is Biscarrosse, Northern Landes. Lots of paddling against rips, some absolute classic days on perfect sandbanks, endless beaches facing vast forests...But I was stoked to move away from that monotony and settle down on 35km long Côte Basque with a mix of decent beachbreak, quality reef and point-breaks. My home is Guéthary now, a tiny 13 sq.meter flat right on the harbour slip. About 50 steps from the paddling point to Parlementia, a long right halfway in between San Onofre and Sunset Beach, or Alcyons / Avalanche, well-shaped lefts holding up to 18ft surf. Set-up is magic when conditions are firing but water is often murky, surface littered with trash and wildlife is almost non-existent.

Northern Spain, since 1989.

mundaka & secret spots.

My first encounter with Mundaka was a magic February week with 7 straight days of 3-12ft flawless surf with little crowd. Now Mundaka is often a zoo but one classic barreling wave there makes the trip worth it. I've been trying to hit Mundaka once every winter now but I tend to favor remote spots on big to huge swells, south winds and midday low tides. Involving long walks through green meadows with sheep, tricky cliff access and shallow rocks. Most of those spots work 5-10 times a year but that's my privilege of proximity.

Dan Merkel is the only non-Australian photographer in this series, showing his dedication to travelling the globe and adding a Hawaiian time capsule to our archives.

one. Hawaiian scene. two. The highly influential Larry Bertleman.

three. Hawaiian legends/pioneers.

switchfoot:gallery

A collection of photographs, art and images from the friends of switch-foot including:

> dickHOOLE

> nigelARNISON

> georgeGREENOUGH

> harryCROCKETT-DAILY

> andrewKIDMAN

> markSUTHERLAND

> ryanHEYWOOD

> darynMcBRIDE

> garyBIRDSALL

> justin&peterCRAWFORD

Photo: nigelARNISON

alexKNOST by: ryanHEYWOOD

Photo: dickHOOLE

if you can

RHV·386

Holiday ©

switchfoot:gallery

Photo proofsheet: dickHOOLE

Photo: peterCRAWFORD

Photo: justinCRAWFORD

Photo by: peterCRAWFORD

switchfoot:gallery

Photo by: peterCRAWFORD

Photo: greg the EGG

kiwi surfer/board-designer/artist/father of triplets
darynMcBRIDE

switchfoot:gallery

' tis always morning somewhere in the world.' [richardHERRYhorne]

Film strips by: dickHOOLE (This is MP at Kirra, pre auto-focus)

switchfoot:gallery

www.litmus.com.au

andrew kidman

Photo: dickHOOLE

The Truth Transcends Time

Looking through Australian surfing history it is tough to find many words on Peter Drouyn and how he fits into the big picture, but he does. It is a simple story really; a story of one man's fight for acceptance in a world that doesn't embrace individuality or eccentricity.

Many will think of Peter Drouyn as the entrepreneurial surfer that introduced the man-on-man competitive system at the first stubbies contest in 1977, the most successful event in surfing history. Some will remember Drouyn as the controversial character in surfing that has always been in the shadows, mostly due to his outspoken ways. Drouyn (the sole Queenslander) who didn't receive the media exposure from the then based Sydney magazines. Drouyn the outsider, the loner, the performer, flamboyant Drouyn, the frustrated entrepreneur, the arrogant Queenslander, the actor, the man that changed the face of modern professional surfing, the Mickey Dora of Australian surfing, the outspoken rebel, the whinger, call him what you will. Drouyn is a controversial character, not liked by many, yet idolised by a core that could see his vision. Fact: Drouyn was a pioneer for Queensland surfing and the further I got into this puzzle the more interesting it became.

Drouyn will acknowledge that by the age of 11, he was an outsider with a vivid imagination and not accepted by his peers. Drouyn took these personal problems to the ocean and developed a radical style of surfing that was to help take surfing into a new generation of power surfers, but he was never to get much credit for his achievements. Drouyn has a successful surfing career; he was a visionary and always has been. Drouyn's surfing was futuristic at a time (mid 1960's), when Sydney surfers were expected to be futuristic not some lone individual from Queensland. Queensland was 'no-mans land' in the mid 1960's (amazing how much things can change) and Australian surfing was a Sydney (NSW) based activity that had several of the world's best surfers (eg Nat and Midget) and domination on the surfing media; the media that Drouyn still resents to this very day. Asking Drouyn about his bitterness towards the media he said the following;

Drouyn: "There's no doubt they cut me wings off, they tried to turn me into a dodo. Then the dodo couldn't fly, but he kept growing his wings back, and they would just chop them off again until the dodo gave up and was happy walking."

Resentment aside, this story outlines the truth, not only about Drouyn's surfing but also his vision for competitive surfing, a vision that was way ahead of its time. The mid 1960's were a crazy time in surfing. It was new, it was exciting and everything was happening so fast that if you went away for a few weeks you came back to something entirely different. Competitive surfing was primitive and biased with its judging, surfboards were heavy logs built for nose riding; yet there were young surfers, like Drouyn, pushing for more performance boards. This was the era where surfing was either going to go down the competitive road or the artistic road and we all know what happened, a natural human competitive instinct filtered into surfing too.

Peter Drouyn

Drouyn SURFING:

Photo: malSUTHERLAND

At the age of 15 (1965) Drouyn was the Queenslander to really push for competitive results on a national level, although Russell Hughes and Bob Mctavish had already made inroads into the NSW psyche. This was the time, the era, when competitive surfing really got moving and Drouyn had the competitive drive. No one thought he could do it. No one thought he could compete with the dominance of the NSW surfers. Drouyn believed in Drouyn, in fact, he had so much belief in himself that this was fairly perceived as arrogance, especially considering that Drouyn had no profile as a surfer, and Queensland had not registered in the surfing world. Drouyn developed a support group around him, a support group that contained himself, his own self-confidence/ego and his own skill...

Drouyn: "It was just a mask to keep the spirits up. I had to promote a self-confidence that could overcome the ego thing of the New South Welshmen. I got into a lot of blues (fights) and everything to prove that I could do it."

Drouyn travelled down to Sydney for the Australian titles (1965 aged 15), with an air of confidence that was not received well by the New South Welshmen (NSW). Drouyn was the lone soldier from Queensland. It wasn't a very welcome visit from the confident Queenslander, who believed he had the skill to beat Kevin 'The Head' Brennan (who was at that time touted as being unbeatable after winning both the NSW Junior and senior titles.) For those of you who know your history, you know what transpired. Drouyn, aged 15, was beaten up and found in a pool of blood (by Bob Evans) and taken to hospital. Fortunately the doctors managed to stitch him up and Drouyn paddled out with a revolutionary watertight bandage around his head and he won the Australian Junior title (1965), with Midget winning the opens. Drouyn put Queensland on the map. What a great story it makes. It is a story of natural progression for Queensland surfing and one that had to be made. The fact that Peter Drouyn was leading this transcendence, did not help his cause. First impressions last and Drouyn has been an outsider within surfing ever since.

PT: "Drouyn was like TROY you know...he would go down and do gladiatorial battle with the New South Welshmen, and he was the only one from Queensland! He was the lone soldier doing battle with Nat and Midget and Ted (Spencer) and so I think he's not at times given the credit for how really great he was you know, I mean he really was. Drouyn was the one that gave Qld surfing its first level of respect, but he had to fight for it."

You were one of the only Queenslanders going down there (New South Wales) for the competitions; did you experience much resentment from the New South Welshmen?

Drouyn: "You know... complete resentment. I mean it was 'How dare you come down here with your head up high and confident?' ...And having skill as well AND being a Queenslander (being sun bronzed and them being white skinned), I had all this other stuff. It was the kingdom of jealousy that I entered. I wasn't ever going to take a step back though, because if you take a step back then your dream starts to crack you know. I think I told them 'I will do well, I'll do well, I'll do really well' and of course I got beaten up...but that didn't stop me."

1965 and surfing was based in Sydney (along with all the media) and Queensland (in general) was not given the exposure that it may have deserved and it wasn't until the next generation of Queenslanders (Rabbit, MP and PT) came through that the New South Wales dominance of surfing (and the media) ended. But this was too late for Drouyn... Up against a team of New South Welshmen that had surfers, surfing culture, media and infrastructure (that was all geared up towards NSW dominance) Drouyn, with his air of confidence, was on the outside looking in.

PT: "Drouyn was probably one of the most under-rated surfers of that generation, because he lived in Queensland and the Queenslanders were not given due credit for how good they were surfing... and their surfing had evolved (because of the quality of the waves) and Drouyn was the frontrunner."

Paul Neilsen: "Peter, while being serious about his surfing and a fierce competitor has always maintained a great sense of humour. I'll never forget our first road trip to the Bells Beach Easter contest in the mid sixties, it's almost worth a book in itself. Also anyone who was at the recent ASAQ's 40th Anniversary and heard his poem about the people and events of those 40 years will no doubt wholeheartedly agree that Peter has a seriously funny side."

Midget: "He didn't have the promotional group behind him like Nat had. He had to do what he did by himself to a degree, because he was isolated in Queensland. "

An outstanding talent that was pushing Malibu riding into unchartered territory; surfing the hollow perfect waves of Burleigh Heads and Kirra, Drouyn naturally developed a different style of surfing to the Sydney based surfers. Using Mickey Dora, Phil Edwards and Joey Cabell as a template Drouyn was an aggressive/stylish cat from a very early age and still is today.

In 1965, after the Australian Junior titles (where Drouyn had just beaten the stylish/futuristic Kevin 'The Head' Brennan) Drouyn was back in Queensland verbalising that he would win again in 66'. Even in Queensland, Drouyn wasn't liked for his confidence and immediately forced himself into loner status...with support only coming from his mother and father and his shapers (Gold Coast shaping mentor) Laurie Hohensee...and later, Bob McTavish.

Did your confidence grow after beating the unbeatable Kevin Brennan in the 1965 Australian titles?

Drouyn: 'Of course. If you achieve a notion that you can beat someone who is portrayed as Goliath and you can pick the weaknesses and you know the limitations of surfing manoeuvres at the time, and you are going beyond those (and you're not seeing anyone going beyond those in the photos or the movies) well surely that's going to give you confidence. But no one told me I was going beyond it because there was a lot of jealousy around, a lot of ego. It was a bit like when Cassius Clay beat Sonny Liston...he was one of my heroes Cassius Clay... Kevin Brennan was a lovely surfer."

In 1965, Midget Farrelly was synonymous with the word surfing in Australia and around the world. Midget had Nat Young, Kevin Brennan, Bobby Brown and Drouyn all challenging for the top position in surfing. With the tragic deaths of both BB and Brennan, it seemed it was either going to be Drouyn or Nat that would take the mantle and all the trimmings that go with it. Drouyn, the Queenslander, was outspoken and controversial and not part of the 'scene'...the writing was on the wall.

Tony Dempsey: "Drouyn was the first guy knocking down barriers; he forcibly introduced Queensland surfing to the rest of Australia."

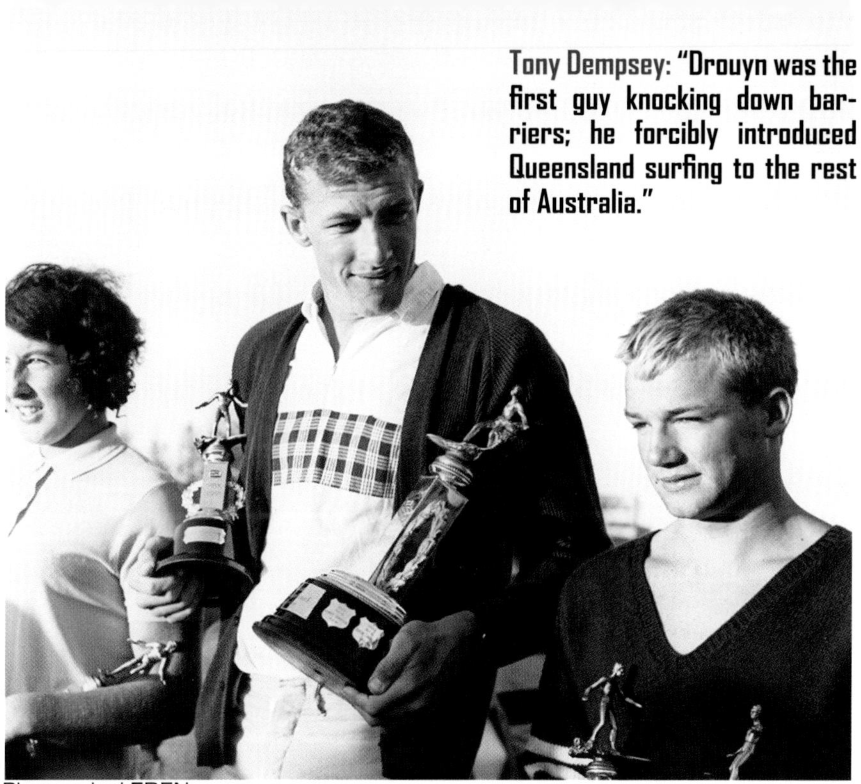

Photos: jackEDEN

Drouyn

Photos: dickHOOLE

CHRONOLOGY

1965: Qld Junior Champion
Australian Junior Champion

1966: Qld Junior Champion
Australian Junior Champion

1967: 2nd Qld Titles (Graham Black)
R/U Australian titles and runner up at Bells (winner Nat Young)
3rd in the Makaha International (aged 17) behind Joey Cabell and Fred Hemmings

1968: Won Qld Titles
Favoured to win the Australian titles, but was injured
Caught pleurisy at Puerto Rico World titles

1969: Won Qld Titles
R/U Australian titles (winner Nat Young)
National surf club individual men's champion (beating Ted Spencer and Michael Peterson)

1970: Qld Champion
Australian Men's Champion
Makaha International champion
2nd Duke (winner Jeff Hackman)
4th Smirnoff
3rd at Peruvian international championships (winner Rolf Aurness)
Voted number one surfer in the World by Hawaiian Surfing Association

1971: R/U Australian titles

Photos: dickHOOLE

Retired from competitive surfing

1972: R/U Bells

1973: National Institute of Dramatic Art, the movie Drouyn with Bob Evans, and also posed nude for Cleo magazine!

1974: Attempted to make a comeback in surfing with R/U at Bells to MP

1975: R/U Pa Bendall contest (winner Michael Peterson)
5th Australian titles

1976: Begins working with Stubbies

1977: The first Stubbies contest (won by MP) the most successful surfing contest in the history of surfing
Drouyn was running third in the World title race in 1977 (even though he didn't compete in the Stubbies which he organised) then wasn't invited to the Duke contest in Hawaii. Drouyn finished 5th in the World title race that year, his last year as a real competitor.
R/U Bells

Drouyn

SHORTBOARD REVOLUTION

Bob McTavish: "I'd say Drouyn was the first high profile surfer to push hard for Lightweight (1965). I'd go further than that, and say he was frustrated with the whole concept of surfboards at the time...he was truly ready for the shortboard revolution of the next year before anyone."

Drouyn's charge in the Australian titles continued in 1966, although this year he was even more impressive than during his win the year before. At his home break in Coolangatta Queensland, surfing again in the juniors, many believe that Drouyn should have surfed in the opens in 66', and what a great contest it would have been against Nat Young, who won the seniors.

"Junior finalist Peter Drouyn looked up, grinned and power he did. He surfed with a grace and power that not only won him his second National Junior Championship but also annihilated his opposition. He surfed with a style that signalled the end of N.S.W domination of the Australian surf scene. He displayed the best of a Queensland brand of surfing that might be summed up with one word, power, and this is the basic reason for the Queenslander's stunning performance in the 1966 Nationals. Drouyn surfed the way he wanted to surf and if the wave crumbled, that was too bad – for the wave, he powered it into submission." (Lester Brien, Surfing World 1966)

Bob McTavish shaped Drouyn's board for the titles that year and he shaped it lightweight. Drouyn kept saying he wanted it shorter and lighter. This was a new concept at the time and led by Drouyn in 1966.

McTavish: "I must admit, I could have overlooked a few things with Drouyn in my recall of history, but I do know for sure that in 1966, that is pre-revolution, Drouyn was pushing for change. I shaped him the board he won the Aussie juniors on in 1966 and he wanted it light light light, which we did, we only did a single glass job. He wanted to be able to bottom turn like you wouldn't believe and I made the mistake of making the tail too wide, still thinking Malibu style then you know. So...Drouyn was pushing hard in 66', he was the best surfer in the water, Nat was second best."

This is a pretty big call from McTavish, especially as Nat was world champion in 1966. When I asked Bob if he was sure he wanted this to go to print he said the following;

McTavish: "That's how I saw it. Drouyn was scarily good... He had all Nat's moves down, but he had more class, more polish and a better-looking package. Of course, after that with the advent of the shortboard, and with Nat's opportunities and support team, Nat emerged again as the leader..."

Drouyn: "We were in the shaping bay for half a day working on that board and in the end it came out perfectly. I knew what I wanted and thanks to Bob he let it happen."

So this is where the truth came out about Drouyn's involvement with the Shortboard Revolution. While based in Queensland Drouyn was not in the media spotlight at all, he was off the radar. The Sydney based surfers were right in the thick of it and consequently Australian surfing history has overlooked Drouyn's importance from this era and no doubt others. Drouyn was emotional when I told him (over the phone) that McTavish had finally laid some credit on him for his involvement in the period of the revolution. Drouyn was so relieved to have his sanity restored/authenticated more than anything else. As the story goes, in 1965 Drouyn was literally in tears begging the then glasser (John Mantle) to do one layer of glass to bring the weight down.

McTavish: "Yes, I'd say Drouyn was the first high profile surfer to push hard for Lightweight. I'd go further than that, and say he was frustrated with the whole concept of surfboards at the time...he was truly ready for the shortboard revolution of the next year before anyone... Nat was happy with the "involvement" era that was a big enough step for him at the time 1966... I certainly wish Drouyn was in Sydney when it all came down in '67... and I secretly think Peter wishes he was there too...along with Ted, Baddy, Kevin Platt, Midget, Keith..." "So tyranny of distance kicked in for poor Peter, who was as hot as Nat or Ted, and just as eager for the change... actually, MORE eager, as Nat was missing in celebrity-land for the first few months of the revolution."

Nat Young: "It is fine to say that Drouyn was one of a bunch of extremely talented surfers pushing hard, including *Ted Spencer and Wayne Lynch*... they were all a fair bit younger than me."

1966 World Titles in San Diego: The only reason Drouyn surfed the Australian juniors again (in 1966) was that he knew there was a junior World Title up for grabs later in the year and he needed to qualify...and qualify he did...BUT, the 'powers to be' cut the junior event from that World titles in 1966 and Drouyn was left to surf his first senior event, in the World titles in San Diego. Unfortunately for Drouyn, the board that McTavish had shaped him had snapped and he didn't manage to get the right board for his style of surfing. Drouyn nearly made the open men's final aged 16 (as an unknown Australian kid) with little support from his fellow countrymen/judges because he was an outsider. It took Drouyn until his trip to Hawaii in 1967 where he came 3rd in the Makaha International before he got another surfboard that he really excelled on, a board shaped by Bill Fury/Dick Brewer with McTavish waiting in the wings ready to saw off the tail of anything over 9 foot! (In 1968 Drouyn started shaping his own boards on the Gold Coast, because he couldn't find anyone to shape what he wanted).

Fred Hemmings: "As surfing was evolving into rock and roll in the mid 60's and early 70's, Peter helped it find a good riff. Peter was a rock and roller, he wasn't interested in waltzing with the waves like I was. As far as his surfing goes, he was very progressive for his time, innovative in helping change surfing in Hawaii and Australia from a classic style to rock and roll." (from 'The Missing Link' PLB)

Drouyn

THE LATE 1960'S

Drouyn: "Primarily I'm a surfer and I'd like to be remembered for the major contribution which was this thing called 'power surfing' because I can't think of anyone who began it before me other than the concepts of Mickey Dora. I was the first one to be doing that, riding a long board like a shortboard, with power and aggression."

Photos: eddieSAWDEN and malSUTHERLAND

1967 was Drouyn's first year in the open men's Australian Titles and no doubt there was a buzz in the air as to whether this kid could actually beat Nat Young. In the following quote by Bob McTavish, you can feel what McTavish thought of his chances against Drouyn.

McTavish: "In the Qld titles I only ever competed myself 3 times (64, 65, 66) and the Australian titles twice then I quit because Drouyn became a senior then, so I was out of there, because Drouyn was too good hahaha, he was a junior before that."

Mal Sutherland: "It's no news that Peter is bitter about the treatment he received from the surf media and others at the time, and rightly so, though I must say he brought a lot of it on himself with his sledge hammer approach. Then again others before him (and the advent of competition surfing) had tried to convince the NSW surf mafia that we had a number of surfers here in Queensland that were better than some of those being promoted in the magazines and movies, with no success, so maybe his approach was the right one. To say that Drouyn was the first to gain attention to surfers for Queensland is probably wrong as Russell Hughes and McTavish were well known and respected, though they had to go to Sydney to work to receive that recognition. Drouyn was the first not to have to relocate."

Nat Young in 1967 was unstoppable and on top of the world, but all reports I collected are that this kid from Queensland really made people take notice, especially after two successive national junior titles. At Bells Beach, Drouyn in his first national title surfing in the opens and again he was very impressive, but not impressive enough to convince the judges that he had beaten the world champion. Midget was third in 1967 and the next few years looked promising for some serious competition. *In Hawaii*, Drouyn came third in the *Makaha International* in 1967 (aged 17) behind Joey Cabell and Fred Hemmings, an event that he would later go on to win.

People started to notice Queensland (in general) and Drouyn was the frontrunner in this power style of surfing ...taken to a new level by the next generation of Queenslanders and particularly Michael Peterson (MP). Hearing what they said about Drouyn was encouraging...

PT: "Drouyn inspired me. I learnt something important from Drouyn early on... that you really need to be a star too, as well as surfing well in the water...YOU NEED TO BE A STAR TO MAKE IT. It was his personality and his aura. And even today when you're around him he still has that aura."

Rabbit: "What Drouyn showed me was; he created his own aura. He had an aura about him. He was this charismatic person I really studied that. It was certainly something I put in my little quiver of arrows. I said that's one for me right there. I really observed Drouyn very closely."

Drouyn: "I wasn't aware of any of that back then. I mean obviously now in hindsight yeah. Look, I struggled to the surface of the ground like some frustrated rat, who was trying to get to the top of the ground to breathe air (for some reason) and the hole that I made and struggled with was left there for others I guess..."

Many remember Peter Drouyn as the individual that introduced the man on man competitive system and the Stubbies surf contest. Aside from your competitive results, what would you like people to remember Peter Drouyn as?

Drouyn: "Primarily I'm a surfer and I'd like to be remembered for the major contribution which was this thing called 'power surfing' because I can't think of anyone who began it before me other than the concepts of Mickey Dora. I was the first one to be doing that, riding a long board like a shortboard, with power and aggression."

1968 and Drouyn was getting fired up to win the 1968 Australian titles, but he couldn't compete, as he was injured. The late Keith Paull won and this was the first time Nat or Midget had not taken the title in the 1960's. Keith Paull is another great surfer and shaper that many kids today probably know nothing about. His achievements will be remembered, particularly his surfing and design. (Rest In Peace).

Also around late 1967/early 1968 Wayne Lynch (from Victoria) was starting to shine through and win senior events and again, another surfer that was one of the visionaries pushing for change.

By the year of 1969 Drouyn was reaching the peak of his competitive career, some say he was the best surfer in the world at this time... Drouyn felt really uncomfortable talking about the 1969 Australian titles that were held in Western Australia. He knows he won the final, but it was Nat again who won the title on a decision that still upsets Drouyn to talk about. After talking to a few 'older' surfers around, many still talk of how Drouyn was 'ripped off in 69'.' By 1970 it seems that no one was going to stop Drouyn and no one did. He was finally the Open men's Australian champion. It was around this time that Queensland began it's dominance of the Australian titles for many years to follow.

PT: "Drouyn won that Australian title at Greenmount Point (1970). A couple of years after that you know the Queenslanders took over, at Narrabeen. There was like 5 out of the 6 finalists in the Australian titles, at Narrabeen NSW (in their fricken backyard)... were from Queensland!!!"

How good did it feel to finally win the Australian title in 1970?

Drouyn: "There is controversy everywhere too. The 1970 title was a relief more than anything because it was just getting to the point where I felt it was getting taken from me for no reason there for a few years. It just seemed that the odds were so against them letting me win it even on my own ability. In 1970 I said, 'this is it, if they find a way to cut me out of it this year I am going to give it away.' I went the hardest I have ever gone, shaped my own board for it and you know it was 4-5 rounds or something, I led every round and even at the end they (NSW) wanted another round just to try and peg me back."

Drouyn: "Every time I go surfing I have a party on my own, and when I come in I'm uplifted because everyone else around me are dead people walking."
photos: dickHOOLE

Drouyn

1970

Drouyn was at his peak competitively and perhaps he never again reached those heights of the late 1960's and particularly 1970 when he was voted the number one surfer in the World by the Hawaiian Surfing Association.

carmel - keithPAULL - johnMANTLE - randyRARRICK - peterDROUYN (in Hawaii)

Photo: unknown

Photo: laurieMcGUINESS

In 1970, coming off a very successful season in Hawaii where Drouyn won the Makaha International, placed second in the Duke and 4th in the Smirnoff, some say that Drouyn should have gone on to win the world title that year (1970) at Johanna and Bells Beach, but he didn't have the right board. Drouyn snapped his 7"10' leading up to the event and had to settle for his 5"10' in large swells. The winner, Rolf Aurness, had an extensive quiver with boards up to 8 feet long. Drouyn wasn't the only one riding the wrong board though. 1970 was a time when surfers really were experimenting heavily with how short they could go with their boards. Even Nat Young rode a board under 6 feet long in those world titles, in big surf!

Rabbit: "The 1970 world title was the one, in my opinion, for him to win. It would have been huge if he had won it. It would have been one of those things where he would be remembered as a world champion. He was so dominant in the Australian titles that year at Greenmount Point."

Some people say you should have won the World title in 1970 but you had the wrong board for the conditions down there in Victoria. What do you say to that?

Drouyn: "Yeah I did, I blew it. I blame myself for that. It was the wrong board. To tell you the truth I was short on resources, my comeback machine broke in half about a month before the contest and that was 7"10' and that was the one to win it. I ended up taking out the bloody 5"10' and yeah I needed a bigger board."

It might have been the end to a really incredible run for Drouyn. From 1965 until 1970 Drouyn was at his peak competitively and perhaps he never again reached those heights of the late 1960's and particularly 1970 when he was voted the number one surfer in the World by the Hawaiian Surfing Association. Drouyn's aggressive surfing in Hawaii along with his flamboyant surfing on the point breaks in Queensland he is the complete surfer. Even today Drouyn is still surfing unbelievable and you can hear the grommets in the line-up asking, 'who is that guy?' as Drouyn charges down and around the line on some futuristic board he has shaped himself. Drouyn still wonders what it would have been like if he was part of the system and grew up in Sydney...who would have been the individual Queenslander attempting to join the 'circle' and become one of the best surfers in the world?

Rabbit: "The flamboyance of Drouyn... The no paddle take offs behind the rocks at Snapper, the full defiance, he surfed with defiance; he surfed with a certain arrogance. That really appealed to me. It was like a matador approach really. He surfed Kirra like a matador."

PT: "One of the most remembered images of me is the shot taken right out front here at the Coolangatta shore break (taken by Martin Tullemans) of the soul arch with the hands above my head.... and Drouyn used to do that in the 60's! AT KIRRA! You know...and it's more like a matador in a bullfight..."

I don't know if you know that Rabbit and PT both describe Drouyn as like a matador with the cape? That's how they describe you.

Drouyn: "There you go, well there you go. Actually I had one of the famous Spanish bullfighters, a big picture of him framed from about 1962 (on my wall), I felt this bullfighter, the way he stood there and he had his chest up high, neck straight and his back perfectly straight...he had his cape out in front and the BULL was like a toy! And he had so much control and there's this huge dangerous thing attacking him and his face was just completely at rest and totally concentrated and I thought that represented my style and that was me too, but with surfing."

What would you say to the comment that some people describe Peter Drouyn as the Mickey Dora of Australian Surfing?

Drouyn: "It would be very accurate I suppose. First of all, as I evolved and you've got your heroes and Mickey Dora (at one stage) was my absolute God. I wore his board shorts, colours...I loved his style, I learnt to side slip from him off an old Grant Rohloff film...I thought this guy is unbelievable...HE is doing things which is actually very much power type surfing. In fact it was Mickey Dora who started 'power surfing' if you like. Then I just took that and the personality and a bit of aggression and took it to another level."

Did you ever meet Dora?

Drouyn: "Yeah God amazing. I met him about 3 months before he died; we had lunch together in France. We got on like wildfire. Mickey even said to me 'Peter how do I look, do I look younger than 65?' I said 'You look fine Mickey.' That was quite incredible, he was my hero and I finally met him before he died, it was quite strange."

Dora is pretty famous for a few things he has said, do you have a moment of inspiration now for a Drouyn quote that people might remember you for?
(At this stage Drouyn pauses for a while)

Drouyn: "Every time I go surfing I have a party on my own, and when I come in I'm uplifted because everyone else around me are dead people walking."

Drouyn has ideas, innovation and intrigue just pouring out of him. I was not surprised when he came up with this quote. Having your glass half empty as some describe Drouyn...but the following is just plain sad.

I heard you recently sold all your trophies and even the board you won the Oz title on. Was that a ceremonious thing or did you really need the cash?

Drouyn: "Yes I was pretty desperate; I needed the cash because I went back to university and did law. I didn't have much in reserve anyway, so I had to sell all my...it was terrible I hated doing it and I hope one day soon I can buy some of it back...especially my Makaha Championship bowl."

Photo: dickHOOLE

Drouyn

THE STUBBIES: Drouyn talks

Drouyn did rise to the top of Australian surfing; he even rose to great heights in Hawaii. It seems futile that Drouyn basically quit surfing competitively when he finally got there (1970). He finally won the Australian titles, he had a profile worldwide then he threw it all away for a career in acting. Enrolling in the National Institute for Dramatic Art (NIDA) and then completing the big screen movie project titled 'DROUYN" in 1973 with good mate Bob Evans, competitive surfing didn't see much of Drouyn in the early 1970's.

Drouyn was busy working with Stubbies management to create a surfing contest that would end up changing the face of modern professional surfing.

Michael Peterson (Winner): "I thought it was a very well run contest and I give a lot of credit to Peter Drouyn for his new system. It is a great idea that there is money from the last competitor right the way through."

Mark Richards (2nd Place): "It was definitely the best contest I have ever surfed in, by far. It was the first contest that was a surfing ability contest not a hassling ability contest. With only two people in the water there's no way you can complain about being hassled. I think Drouyn should run every contest! With the one on one system you have to surf much better than you do with six people in the water. With six people, they take the first three, and all you have to do is qualify, you don't have to win, but with one against one you have to win."

Shaun Thomson: "Drouyn's man on man judging system, in my mind, is the best judging system ever developed for surfing contests. It worked perfectly at Burleigh Heads. There were two of us out there at a time, battling it out in the Burleigh Barrels, what more could a spectator ask for?"

(All quotes from 'The Wave Game' by Phil Jarratt a Tracks Publication circa 1977)

THE STUBBIES: Drouyn talks

Photo of mp: dickHOOLE

How long did take you to organise the stubbies?

Drouyn: "It was based on 15 years of looking at and competing in surfing contests. I'd never really felt right about the way the winner had been chosen and this was my chance to put it all together. The Stubbies Company paid for all the logistics and all the revolutionary sort of structures I had in mind. They approached me to do the thing, they were going broke and they wanted to restore their business and I said I would do the Stubbies board-shorts and the contest at Burleigh. They wanted the contest at Sydney and I said, 'forget that shit.' We had around 20, 000 people a day at that contest (over ten days), the gate didn't exist after a while... there were so many people."

After the 1977 stubbies (that was the most successful contest in surfing's history) how did you not get the job to keep your vision alive?

Drouyn: "Stubbies ended up huge. After that event they became a multi-million dollar company. When the Sales Manager became the boss... 'He cut me throat.' That was it mate, I was totally cut from that success story. I wish I was a bloody lawyer then."

Many people in the surfing industry talk of your next phase to the man-on-man framework; the wave stadiums, can you explain this to us?

Drouyn: "Well the man-on-man was the first phase...getting two blokes in the water instead of 6. The next phase was the Checkmate Challenge Cup and it was based on a tennis match format...where each wave is like a point in a tennis match and the match goes over 'facts do not cease to exist because they are ignored.' [aldousHUXLEY]

Photos: merkel

Photo: peterCRAWFORD

3 sets with the crowd getting involved with the judging. Two surfers in the water and they both catch a wave and after they have both caught a wave the judges decide who goes to '15 love' and so on..."

Drouyn: "The wave stadiums I did a patent for in 1979, it was meant to take us into stadiums with waves and have us (surfers) independent of Surf Companies and create our own corporate sponsorship. Revenue into the stadiums would pay the surfers and they would be under a contract much like football clubs today... So that these clothing manufacturers wouldn't have all this power...I mean they would still be involved, they could still get contracts with the surfers, but they would be separate."
"Wave stadium surfing; you would have teams fighting against each other; you'd have the Gold Coast Dolphins against the Sydney Snakes for example. And of course that would involve rock bands, half time, free surfing...anyway I put it to Rip Curl, Quicksilver and that sort of thing and then there was a spate of people building wave pools which were just a very primitive form of what I was on about. That's where it all sort of stopped and then it just went back to the ocean and here it is now you know."

In 1984 Drouyn organised a man-on-man with the then unbeatable MR and in the contest the two surfers rode single fins, twin fins, thrusters, 4 fins and mals. Now there is another Drouyn idea/format that is way ahead of it's time!

Drouyn: "I was out in the cold after the first stubbies.I was ignorant. I thought people would have to support me after I was so successful."

Drouyn

REFLECTIVE: conversations with Drouyn (circa 1980)

Peter Townend has kindly allowed me to reprint some extracts from his story titled 'Conversations with Peter Drouyn." This was written in 1980 and I feel these extracts shed some light on how Drouyn was in 1980. This is 3 years after he introduced the man-on-man judging system at the first Stubbies in 1977.

PT: "In 1971 surfing magazine did a classic interview with you called "Drinks at the bar in 1979" and you say some things that were futuristic at the time. Do you think far too futuristic seeing 1979 has come and gone?"
Drouyn: "Maybe I was prophesizing something that I would do in the late 70's, but not knowing really what I would do. When I did "Drinks at the Bar," I was thinking if nobody else did anything, maybe DROUYN would, and it happened in 1977. I thought, if it happens in '77, in two years if they keep on the right track, in '79 we'll all be drinking at the bar, our own clubs, our own social places. We'll all have heaps of bread, we'll have copyrights all over ourselves; we'll be protected from the media and the public and from ourselves. After the first stubbies, it didn't go on the right track. The wrong people got hold of it, they raped it, and they're using it. It is such a shame – we've gone back to 1970."

PT: "Were there any people in surfing that you would have considered heroes?"
Drouyn (1979): "Mickey Dora, Joey Cabell, Phil Edwards, Johnny Fain, Dewey Webber, Midget, Kemp Aaberg. There are others, but those guys mainly, especially Dora, Edwards and Joey Cabell. Those three, they were my heroes, but in a different way. They were my heroes because they were rebels and because – partly to do with my escapism – I became a rebel, an outcast on my own. I wanted to kill the world; I wanted to get on top of it, get on top of myself." "I found that Dora had the kind of rebellion that I needed to follow, Cabell had the aggro and the killer instinct, while Edwards had the style and the beauty and the couldn't-give-a-damn attitude in contests. I combined those three and it really helped me."

"To me, Bob Evans ('Evo') is the hero of Australian surfing. He's the man who started everything. He started international surfing. He was an adventurer – a real, true Australian adventurer, a man who had nothing and went for the dare. He took Drouyn along because I was the only guy who would dare to go with him. Drouyn wasn't a yes-man. Evo hated yes-men, although Evo had to go along with Witzig and that bullshit era, because Evo was making money through that. Evo stood aside and said I am taking Drouyn – not Nat or Midget or Wayne, or Ted or Keith; it was Drouyn. God I really appreciate him for that."

PT: "I notice you have come to this surf contest and you have brought one surfboard, which is a pretty strange looking surfboard. Comment around the beach is that Drouyn has gone nuts and that this board won't work."(The board was an asymmetric setup, with the middle fin not in the centre of the board, a direction surfcraft built for riding only left hand waves.)
Drouyn: "For sure, exactly. They have been saying that for so many years. Drouyn was nuts when he said he could win the New South Wales, Australian Title; Drouyn was nuts when he put channels into boards in 1968; Drouyn was nuts when he came third in the World Championships on a 5'11" board at Johanna when the surf was over ten feet. Drouyn was nuts when he rode a 9', 20 pound board at Sunset; Drouyn was nuts when

he built a concave noserider; he was nuts when he said he could ride a board with four ounces of cloth on either side. Drouyn was nuts when he performed his Russian exercises on the beach before going into a heat. It's just stupid! Drouyn was nuts when he went man-on-man."

PT: "We were talking about body surfing and you said you went body surfing the other day and you wished that the Surfabout Contest was a body surfing contest."
Drouyn: "I wish it was a body surfing contest, because the judges wouldn't know how to judge it, so I could probably win it. (laughs) right?

PT: "There're people who like to watch Drouyn surf; there're people who like to watch Fitzie surf; there're people who like Nat, Midget, Wayne; there're people who like Mark Richards."
Drouyn: "Exactly, and this is what I am saying. How can you judge a situation like that? How can you? How can you judge him against me if I'm noseriding for 50 yards and Richards is doing slambams for 50 yards? The judges are brainwashed by magazines, movies, and things, and people on the top. Because Richards is the man at the top at the moment, in the limelight, everyone's got to be doing what he's doing."

It is interesting hearing what Drouyn said back then and in many ways it still bears relevance today, perhaps even more so.

'in vino veritas - the truth comes out in wine.' [PLANTUS]

the Truth Transcends Time

Drouyn was an important component to the shortboard revolution, his surfing helped to push the shapers (particularly McTavish) into new ground, through cutting edge surfing and wanting to push the boundaries. Drouyn, growing up surfing waves like Burleigh and Kirra demanded shorter boards not just for the waves but the style or surfer that Drouyn is. While he is given next to no credit for power surfing, I hope this story gives people interested in Surfing's history a bit more of a look at one of the original outsiders, Peter Drouyn.

I will leave you here with some words from Rabbit and PT on Drouyn and say a massive thankyou to all the Elders who helped this story come to life, particularly Bob McTavish, Peter Townend and Rabbit but also Dick Hoole, Nat Young, Jack Eden, Andrew Kidman, Von Weirdo and of course Peter Drouyn.

Rabbit: "The best session I ever saw Drouyn have is one of the best sessions I ever saw anyone have. It was the day he arrived home from Hawaii; he's just won the Makaha international. (Huge event back then in Hawaii). He arrived home and Kirra was just unbelievable, it was so perfect. I'd been surfing it. There was this buzz like..."Drouyn's arrived!" I was like great! I got out of the water, went into the Kirra shed and just sat there and watched this session. This particular session he was going faster than anyone...he was on this unbelievable narrow little board. I'd like to see that board again. It was about 17" wide and it was just a little spear.

The way Drouyn surfed Kirra was just extraordinary, he was just so fast, so brilliant... He was at the absolute apex of his career I reckon, that day. It was something else, something no one has captured. There was nothing captured on film of Drouyn that does him justice, nothing at all. The real stuff he did; the way he surfed Greenmount...the way he surfed Kirra, and obviously the way he surfed Burleigh, it was something I wish they had captured. In my mind's eye, it was extraordinary. I became really conscious of the importance of style in surfing after that day. Drouyn should be remembered as a great Australian surfer."

PT: "Drouyn wasn't afraid to say what he thought. And that sometimes was not to his benefit for sure, but you know beside his own career, being Australian champion and a phenomenally great surfer...pro surfing today owes him a debt of gratitude because the 'Stubbies' changed the face of modern professional surfing."

There is a lot more information, full interview transcripts on the website www.switchfoot.com. with some other interesting questions I asked Drouyn that I couldn't put in here. There is also more information from McTavish talking the shortboard revolution 'moving up a notch in 68' with Ted Spencer's power lines.

If anyone has any photos of Drouyn could you please let me know as I had great difficulty finding any images and even any text and now would be a good time to create a Drouyn archive!

Photo of MP at Backdoor: danMERKEL - circa 1973

'Editors' perspective

Switch-foot was born from frustration...I simply didn't like any of the magazines that were circulating, as all of them focused on the world tour, the competitions and the superstars that they have created. Whilst I have respect for any athlete who can reach the top of their field, surfing has a whole other side to it that is centered on the thrill of the ride, the joy, the stoke, the lifestyle, the music, the culture, the art, the artists, the search, experimentation, respect for nature and a love for the ocean. What you are reading here is my very best effort to put something together that includes as much of the fun side of surfing as possible, with no relevance to the competitive side of surfing.

This is not a history of surfing. This is a collective. Back a few years ago I was having dinner with a mate of mine and he made me realise that I was in the middle of this circle of people within surfing, art and music, and I needed to bring it all together for the greater good of everyone. I set out to do a magazine. I thought it would be finished and on the stands in 6 months.... maybe less. 6 months later I was reading things in the mainstream press that was touching on areas I was focusing on and I had to change my tack...I had to make something that was timeless, and forget the magazine thing...go a different road. Borrowing the money to pay my expenses and spending countless hours on the phone, in the van and on the computer, it started to gather momentum. I knew I was on the right path when I met George Greenough, as his take on surfing was like my take, just multiplied by 40 years of genuine genius perspective. With the collective in mind, this publication gathers together a pool of like-minded individuals into one voice.

The retro movement is alive and expanding, but let us not forget that experimentation has been going on the whole time. However, still today if you asked the average grommet to tell you what George Greenough's significant contributions to surfboard design actually do... the majority would not know. Most modern surfboards don't even include these integral principles. We have all been riding a one-dimensional surfcraft that is spot on for high performance, but way out for the average joe.
Today the whole concept of innovation is receiving exposure in the industry and therefore it is becoming acceptable and commonplace. Five years ago, surfers used to hassle people who were not riding the same board as the world champion, hence people were suppressed into a box of conformation for fear of being alienated. Today, the very people that were criticizing odd boards five years ago are today ordering their 'retro' board from a shaper that probably has no idea how to shape a forward trimming single fin, let alone a Skip Frye styled keel fin fish. These boards are not 'retro', they are current and it is a style of surfing that I choose to call classic surfing...it was alive 40 years ago and it will always be alive. The 'retro revival' is more than just surfcraft though. There is a lot more attention and recognition being given to the fun side of surfing and the surfing 'media pendulum' is swinging away from entirely the competitive realms of surfing, into other areas, and switch-foot is this 'other side of surfing.'

Bearing this paradigm shift in mind, I thought it was a great idea to talk to some 'elders' of surfing, to seek their opinions on surfing in general. Getting to meet some of my surfing heroes and asking them questions that I believed were important, was really special for me and I hope it also inspires you. Slowly uncovering issues within Australian surfing history led to an understanding that I will carry for the rest of my days. As time progresses hopefully there will be more stories like the Peter Drouyn story- one that helps put together the historical archives of our surfing history, particularly around the time of the shortboard revolution.

Also within these pages are the 'legends of the lens,' an honoring of the incredible photographers that so beautifully captured an era of surfing that will never again be experienced. You will notice that there is significant input from the era of pre professionalism (1976) and this is because if you look back to that era you will see that style was everywhere, competitive surfing was in its infancy and innocence was visible in the way surfers rode the waves. Also, it is important that we understand where we have come from and the advice the older surfers pass on really is a life of experience.

While this publication does give a lot of respect back to the generation that pioneered surfing, I have not lost sight of the new school. There is a subculture within surfing that still embraces the goodness of the surfing lifestyle and that is the part of the new school that I have focused on. This is a very real subculture that leads surfing into the future, a sea of individuals with like minds and a common goal. It is the individuals that make the changes. Music, surfing and art seem to fit well and I hope that more people come together through this book, more seedlings sprout to grow this very healthy movement (cheers TC). Right now, with the advent of the Internet, communication is at an all time high and through www.switch-foot.com I hope to help get people involved in what we are passionate about.

On the darker side are the problems of crowded waves, the need for a surfing hierarchy in the line-up and an education of all surfers about the unwritten laws regarding dropping in and not lining up. In many cases, the longboarder paddling around getting more waves than the rest is more of a problem than punters dropping in while you are in the tube. There are people in the water that have no idea about the ocean and treat it like a frothing playground where they can demonstrate their ego to win. Surfing is special, and that attitude should be left on the land. If you are a competitive surfer, then surf like that in your heat but don't instill the com-

switch-foot

petitive attitude on me. Is that preachy? Damn straight it is.

This book is a crack at creating something new within the industry, something that is way over the other side in a left field jungle of creativity with a twist of professionalism. If it had come out five years ago (in Australia) people would have thrown tomatoes at me. I hope you come and find us and check out some of the stuff we are doing, from creating surfing soundtracks to artistic design; switch-foot really is surfing, art and music.

Aside from all the talented contributors, this book would not be here if it wasn't for my mum and her encouragement towards my works and also my doctors for keeping me alive through some very challenging times. I must also thank my father for bringing me up well when I was a kid, and trying to understand me now I am an adult. Also, I could easily write a book about my sole blood brother (James) who came from the depths of despair to fly in the clouds and fathom the horizon, as a pilot.

Thanks to my entire family and particularly my cousin Daniel Crockett who I truly feel was the litmus for my motivation to take a huge step and begin this project. Daniel showed me quality surfing magazines (the journal, surfer's path) at a time when I had not read a modern surfing magazine for over ten years, since the content made me sad. Daniel changed that for me and made me realise that it was possible to represent the fun side of surfing and moreover, that there was a market for it. I think Daniel Crockett is a name that will be with surfing media for the rest of his days.

There are so many names in Australian surfing that haven't featured in here and that is unintentional. What is intended is to put something out that feels good and that is interesting to read. Huge apology to anyone I have upset along the way, if there is anyone who disagrees with what I have represented, please drop me a line.

Thanks to Nigel Arnison for his passion in photography and music, Harry Daily ('Sketch Holiday') for making me slow down and smell the roses, Dick Hoole for giving me a chance when so many other people had ripped him off, Andrew Kidman for being elusive but also being a gardener of the underground surfing culture, Albe Falzon for reminding me of the important things in life, George Greenough for being a beacon of genius simplicity in the midst of a world of thick complexity, Bob McTavish for being one of the fathers of the whole genre of surfing lifestyle, Nat Young for being a straight-shooter with a loud voice in the Tribal Elders story, John Witzig for his amazing photography and immense experience within publishing, Paul Witzig for classic surf films that (God bless him) have not gone digital, Margo for being a country kid, Dane and Belinda for surfing everyday together, Chris Brock for being an underground eternal grommet, Peter Townend for being the style-master, Rabbit for still ripping, Peter Drouyn for being an intellectual futurist, MR for still surfing/shaping, Jack Eden for being old school, Dirk Van Straalen for his open-mindedness and understanding of the way the world really goes around, Thomas Campbell for just being cool, Terepai Richmond for granting me official 'caramel' status, Neal Purchase Jnr for encouraging creativity and being a freakish tube hound, Jamie K for his music magic, Paul Wheat for the 'Kenny club' and his artistic inputs, Shannon Carroll for staying on the good foot and keeping the funk alive, Matt Lye for his music talent, Dain Thomas and Matty Yates for keeping Byron real, the whole crew at the Forster beach house for the beachnik slumber party recordings sessions, Mike and Vic (design) for putting up with my lack of experience, Paul-Jason Rooke (design) for helping to polish this rock into a diamond, Tom and Margie for living the dream, Jake for introducing me, Dave and Hannah for the light, Lucas Wright for being a mediator and source of encouragement, Beno for 'rolling up', Tom Jones for being there and Ross Pelmore for always being there. Peace and God Bless.

AndrewCrockett
ac@switch-foot.com

The team:
Daniel Crockett: dc@switch-foot.com
Shannon Carroll: shannon@switch-foot.com
Dave Rastovich: rasta@switch-foot.com
George Greenough: george@switch-foot.com
Justin Crawford: jc@switch-foot.com
Peter Drouyn: drouyn@switch-foot.com

Cover Art: Harry Daily

Contributing writers: AC and DC or otherwise credited

Contributing photographers: As mentioned throughout the publication

Creative direction: AC

Design layout: Michael Cutts and Vicki Smith
mikecutts@hotmail.com

Image scanning and proof reading: Mac Graphics at Currumbin Valley

Final design, pre-press and photo correction: Paul-Jason Rooke
b.d.a@bigpond.net.au

Broker: John Witzig

Printing and Binding: PH Productions PTE LTD (Singapore)

Distributed by:
Australia: Billabong - the surf company
www.switch-foot.com

SWITCH-FOOT